PLAY IT SAFE

Book Sale

PLAY IT SAFE

The Kids' Guide to Personal Safety and Crime Prevention

by KATHY S. KYTE

Drawings by Richard Brown

Alfred A. Knopf, New York

To Brendon and Brooke with love
and to Rich and Frances with thanks for their help

THIS IS A BORZOI BOOK
PUBLISHED BY ALFRED A. KNOPF, INC.

Text copyright © 1983 by Kathleen Sharar Kyte
Illustrations copyright © 1983 by Richard Brown
All rights reserved under International and Pan-American
Copyright Conventions. Published in the United States by
Alfred A. Knopf, Inc., New York, and simultaneously in Can-
ada by Random House of Canada Limited, Toronto. Distrib-
uted by Random House, Inc., New York.
Manufactured in the United States of America
Book design by Mina Greenstein

5   7   9   10   8   6   4

Library of Congress Cataloging in Publication Data
Kyte, Kathleen Sharar. Play it safe.
Summary: Advice for protecting your home, property, and body
from robbery, assault, and other crimes.
1. Crime prevention—Juvenile literature.   2. Dwellings—
Safety measures—Juvenile literature.   3. Traffic safety
and children—Juvenile literature.   4. Children's rights—Juvenile literature.   [1. Crime prevention.   2. Dwellings—Safety
measures.   3. Safety]   I. Brown, Richard Eric,
1946–   ill.   II. Title.
HV7431.K95   1983   362.8′8   83-6086
ISBN 0-394-85964-2   ISBN 0-394-95964-7 (lib.bdg.)

Contents

Introduction

Any kid, of any age or size, can improve his or her personal safety.

It isn't hard. Crime prevention begins with common sense.

This book will help you take charge of your safety at home and away from home—on the streets, on public transportation, or at school, parks, and other public places. It includes expert advice from police *and* from criminals and gives you sample situations with which to test your safety skills. It tells you how to take a "crook's tour" of your home—checking windows, locks, and doors—and how to make your bike, backpack, and billfold less attractive to thieves.

Educate yourself *about* crime to protect yourself *from* crime. Learn and practice prevention habits to guard yourself and your property and to increase your feelings of confidence and control.

1. ATTITUDE ADJUSTMENT AND BODY ALIGNMENT— Tuning Up for Crime Prevention

"I worry about crime, and I want to do something about it, but I'm only thirteen. What can I do?"

—MARIA

You've probably heard of preventive medicine. It means using sensible exercise, nutritious eating, and a healthy lifestyle to *avoid* medical problems, rather than treating problems after they develop.

You can use the same preventive approach to crime. Your determination to avoid crime and your confidence in yourself can actually protect you from becoming a victim.

In one study, researchers wanted to find out how criminals choose victims and what kinds of "clues" people give that make them likely victims. Convicts at a prison agreed to participate in the study. They were shown a videotape of a real street filled with shoppers, students, business people, and so forth. The convicts were then asked to select "victims"—the people they would be most likely to rob. Ideal victims were shown to be people who appeared to be "out of control," either physically or otherwise. They seemed fearful or preoccupied or were loaded down with purses, packages, and the like. Criminals don't want to have to work for their money. They will automatically pick easy targets—people they can surprise, intimidate, or knock off balance.

Imagine yourself in that videotape. How would you have appeared? Would you have been seen walking and speaking alertly, confidently, and as though you were in control? Or do you need to "tune up" for a better look and a better attitude for increased personal safety?

Attitude Adjustment

"But I'm just a kid," you may say.

"Just a kid." What does *that* mean?

Does being a kid mean that you have fewer rights to your body, your possessions, or your peace of mind than an adult? Of course not. You are as entitled as anyone to a life free from fear, abuse, theft, and injustice.

Does being a kid mean that you're helpless, slow, or hopelessly incompetent? Not if you're like most kids! Most kids are stronger, faster, and more capable than they think. In many cases they are able to outmaneuver, outrun, and outwit a lot of adults.

Respect Yourself

No doubt you're a terrific person. If you want to prove it to yourself, make a list of all your wonderful qualities. No one has the right to victimize such a great kid!

Trust Yourself

Learn to recognize and listen to your instincts—the "gut feeling" you sometimes get that something is not quite right or that someone is not to be trusted. That feeling is like an automatic pilot that can steer you safely away from potentially dangerous situations—but only if you learn to follow it.

For example, Carla thought that the house "looked funny" when she came home from school. A window shade was pulled to one side, and it looked as though the kitchen light was on. Rather than go inside, Carla went to a neighbor's house and phoned a parent, who in turn phoned the police. The police arrived within minutes and arrested two young men who were burglarizing the house.

Many times, people dismiss their gut feelings. They think, "I'm just being paranoid." Well, Carla's "paranoia" protected her from a dangerous situation, and yours could too. Trust and act on your feelings.

Be Alert

Being alert is *not* being paranoid. When you are being alert, you don't assume that everyone (or anyone) is out to harm you. You're just keeping an eye and ear on your world.

Develop the habit of becoming aware of your environment. Most people "tune out" much of the information they receive. You know how that goes. Your *body* is walking down the street, but your *mind* is still at last night's movie or last week's basketball game, or has gone ahead to tomorrow's party. Well, that's okay too. A certain amount of daydreaming is unavoidable and healthy. After all, you can't pay complete attention to every car, truck, pedestrian, house, store, and street. If you tried to do that, a trip to the bus stop would become a major challenge. Still, you need to know where and when you should remain alert—for example, in unfamiliar or high-crime neighborhoods, or when you're out after dark—and you need to "tune in" enough of the time in *any* situation so that you can see, hear, and respond to potential problems. Remember, the

totally tuned-out person is a potential victim. *Looking* alert can protect you.

Getting your attitude together—learning to trust and respect yourself and being alert to your surroundings—is an important first step in playing it safe.

The next step is to use that terrific attitude to bring your body in on the effort to take charge of your safety.

Body Alignment

Body alignment *doesn't* mean you have to turn yourself into a lethal weapon. No one expects you to split logs with the side of your hand or flip someone over your shoulder. Body alignment just means feeling good about, and in control of, the physical equipment you already have. Here are a few exercises to prepare your body for crime prevention.

Front and Center

Find your body's "center." Stand up straight and close your eyes. Imagine a point just below your navel. Open your eyes and practice walking with that point still in your mind. You'll find yourself walking "taller" and with more control, and you'll look more confident.

Balancing Act

Stop walking and stand still. How *do* you stand? Do you usually stand with your feet very close together, with most of your weight on one leg, or leaning against a telephone pole, a building, a bus shelter, or your brother? *Or* do you usually stand with your hands in your pockets? In either case, you look (and are!) out of balance and out of control.

Balance yourself evenly when you stand. Stand straight, feet slightly apart and with your weight evenly distributed over both feet (think of your body's center). Keep your arms at your sides.

To test your balance, try this with a friend: Stand with your feet close together or with all your weight on one leg. Have the friend try to (gently) push you over or knock you off balance. What happens? Try it with your hands in your pockets as if you are leaning against something. You're a pushover! Now, stand "centered"—feet slightly apart, weight evenly distributed—and have your friend try again. Do you see how much harder it is to be thrown off balance when you're centered?

You can build better balance through concentration and practice. Try these three "balance builders":

1. Close your eyes and balance on one leg. Bend down and touch the floor directly in front of the foot that is on the floor. Pretend you're picking up a dime. Now, try it with the other leg.

2. You might have done this balance builder when you were a little kid. Stand on one foot. Grab your raised foot with one of your hands; you'll have to bend your knee to do this. Now, hop in a circle. Try this with your eyes closed.

3. Assume your "balance stance." Lift your right leg and twist your ankle a few times—try turning it in a circle. Do the same thing with your left leg.

Voice Training

Your voice is an important part of your physical equipment. And you can learn to control your voice so it sends clear, confident signals to the world.

Pause a minute and take a breath before you speak. If you run to answer the phone or the door, catch your breath and collect your thoughts so you don't sound breathless—or helpless.

As a rule, you shouldn't speak to strangers, but when it's unavoidable, speak clearly and with control. Don't mumble, mutter, or look away as if you're intimidated. Don't let an answer sound like a question. Keep your conversation brief, don't give *any* personal information, and keep your sentences free of qualifiers. Qualifiers are words and phrases such as "I think," "I guess," "I suppose," and "maybe." Everyone uses qualifiers once in a while, but if you use them frequently, you will sound weak, wishy-washy, and out of control.

Clear, confident speech is not just a personal safety tool. It is also a help in any public speaking situation.

Power Yell

Another thing you can do with your voice is raise it. The best weapon any kid can have is a strong, furious yell. You may never need it, and it is not even advisable to yell in some crime situations, but it is still a valuable tool and one well worth developing.

Criminals, especially rapists, do not expect any sort of aggressive response to their actions. They expect their victims to cry, beg, or at most scream. A yell surprises an attacker and can give a victim time to run away or plan the next response.

A yell is very different from a scream. A scream comes from the throat or the upper chest; it is high-pitched and does not carry very far. A scream is a fear or panic response. A yell comes from the stomach; it is lower-pitched and widely heard. A yell is an anger response. A fierce power yell is the indignant response of a person refusing to be victimized.

This kind of yell takes practice. Find a place to practice some yelling where you won't disturb anyone. If the members of your family support your crime prevention efforts and you live in a private house, they might be willing to put up with—or even participate in—a little basement, barn, or field power yelling. (You'd better warn the neighbors first.) If you live in an apartment, try to get a club, class, or group interested in a crime prevention and personal defense program and find a place to practice power yelling. Maybe you can use the school gym or the park department's recreation room for practice.

"Why bother?" you may ask. "I'll just buy a whistle or get a pocket air horn." These are good ideas too, and a lot of people have them. But remember, they have to be in your hands at *all* times to be useful, and you have to be sure that your hands are free to move the whistle to your mouth or to activate the air horn. An air horn isn't much good if it's in your backpack under your algebra book when you need it. A whistle won't help if you're loaded down with a purse or packages, or if you're grabbed and struggling and can't get it to your mouth.

Another disadvantage of a whistle is that people might not pay attention to it—they might just think it's a kid with a toy whistle. If you *do* decide to carry a whistle or an air horn, carry it in your hand. *Don't* hang a whistle around your neck because it—and you—become too easy to grab.

The two main advantages to a well-practiced power yell are that it is always within "reach" and that it can never be mistaken for anything else. Yelling "No! No! No!" into the face of an attacker clearly shows your determination to avoid victimization. Yelling "Help!" lets others know you are in trouble.

Don't Stop Now

You may want to learn more about personal defense and assertiveness training. Classes in the martial arts or other methods of personal defense are offered in most communities. Some of these classes teach escape skills; others, such as many rape prevention classes, teach skills in fighting back. All stress the importance of confidence, posture, and body awareness, and remaining alert to your surroundings. Classes in personal defense or assertiveness are available at private schools of martial arts, through community colleges or city park departments, and through organizations such as the YMCA, YWCA, YMHA, and the Scouts. Some Girl Scout chapters have begun teaching rape prevention classes to their members. You can also check for classes in your area by phoning your local police or sheriff's office. If you can't find any classes in your community, try to get your club or class (maybe a physical education or health class) interested in bringing someone in to speak about and teach self-defense and assertiveness. There are also good books available, so check your library or bookstore.

Checking It Out

A good attitude and a healthy body are important safety tools. A little education won't hurt either.

How bad *is* crime in your community? Do you really know, or are you just assuming it's bad? Ask the police in your city or town for actual statistics on crimes committed in your area in the past year. Many police departments even have these figures broken down into crimes committed in each neighborhood. You may be surprised to find that the situation is not nearly as bad as you supposed.

It's important, in reading this book, to keep in mind the situation in your community and your neighborhood. All these safety tips make sense for any kid in any area, but some are more appropriate for kids in places with high crime rates.

Keep an eye on your community—crime rates do change—and keep an eye on yourself—your attitude and your body. Be more than just a kid. Be the best and safest kid you can be!

2. HOME SAFE—
Testing Your
"Safety Savvy"

"I don't mind being home alone, but sometimes I get scared, especially at night, and I'm not really sure what I should do if someone calls or comes to the door. I'd like some suggestions so I don't have to worry so much." —DAVID

There's no place like home. There's certainly no place like it for testing your safety skills.

"But I want to relax when I'm home, not look under the bed for bandits," you argue. Besides, you've already skipped ahead to Chapter 6, and you know that your home has safe locks, sturdy doors, and screens on the basement windows. What can go wrong?

Probably nothing. You will probably never have to cope with real situations that are like the sample ones given here, *but* you should know that you *could* cope if you had to. Playing it safe requires advance planning and everyday involvement.

So grab a snack, put up your feet, and check out your home safety skills. No one is going to grade the tests that follow, but some thought and a little common sense should give you an *A* in safety savvy.

Answering the Door

TEST 1

The doorbell rings. You look out a window or through the peephole viewer and see two clean-cut men dressed in well-pressed white uniforms. A van is parked at the curb. *Acme Appliance Repair* is printed on the side of the van. You are not expecting a repairperson. What do you do?

    a. Open the door, leaving the chain on.
    b. Remain quiet and wait for the men to leave.
    c. Call through the door and ask the men what they want.

The play-it-safe answer is c. You should not rely on a chain. Most chains provide poor protection against an intruder. Chapter 6 gives more information about chain locks.

You shouldn't remain quiet either, hoping that the men will go away. You should let them know that someone is inside—and the more people they think are inside, the better. Try this: Call out, loud enough so that they can hear you, "I'll get the door, Dad," then walk to the door and call out through the door, "Yes, can I help you?"

It may sound sexist to pretend that a man—an uncle or your father or another man—is inside with you, and you *can* say, "I'll get the door, Mom." However, you should realize that most criminals are not progressive people, and they are probably more likely to be frightened off by the idea that a man is in the house—even if *your* mother has a black belt in karate.

TEST 2

The repairmen on the porch answer that they have been sent to fix the washer (or dryer or stove or refrigerator or whatever). This is a fairly common ruse. A group in one city recently posed as a natural gas company repair crew, sent to fix a "dangerous leak" in the gas line, and was able to get inside of and burglarize a number of homes before being caught. But let's get back to your repairmen. What do you do next?

    a. Continue to pretend that someone is inside with you and get rid of them.

    b. Phone a neighbor.

    c. Phone a parent.

All three answers are correct. Do all these things, and if the strangers don't leave, phone the police, too!

To get rid of the men, step back from the door and call out loudly, "Dad, the repairmen are here to fix the stove." If that doesn't scare them off, wait a minute, then call out, "Okay, I'll tell them." Through the door, say, "My dad says the stove's fine. It must be a mixup. Drop your card in the mailbox, and he'll phone the shop and straighten things out."

If you don't think you'd be comfortable with all that shouting, you can ask the men—through the door—quietly but clearly what they want, and when they state their business, you can say that you're sorry but your dad's asleep, and if they leave their card in the box, you'll have him call the shop when he gets up.

Think about which version you would be more comfortable saying. Plan and practice it now so that if you ever face a similar situation, you will be well-rehearsed.

TEST 3

Let's change the circumstances a bit. The doorbell rings and two men in work uniforms are on the porch. What would you do if you *were* expecting a repairperson?

   a. Open the door once you've seen their truck, uniform, and tool kits.

   b. Ask them to pass their identification cards through the chained door, and if the cards look okay, let them in.

   c. Have them slip their identification cards under the door or into the mail chute. Look at the pictures carefully. If they look suspicious or you are uneasy, call the repair shop to confirm the repairmen's identification.

The playing-safe answer is *c. Don't* open the door, and *don't* trust the chain until you've looked over the identification cards. And if repairpeople in your community don't carry identification cards, get the person's name and telephone the shop to confirm the identification.

Most of the time, and in most communities, people who claim to be repairpeople *are* repairpeople, but there have been problems in some large cities with burglars pretending to be repairpeople to gain entrance to homes. Even if this has *never* happened in your city or town, you should always be very careful about letting people into your home when you are alone. You should remember that it's *your* home, and it's *your* right and responsibility to keep out any person *you* don't want in. Don't feel self-conscious about refusing to open the door. You're just playing it safe!

Here's another situation: Someone knocks. You look out and see a young woman carrying an enormous bouquet of flowers. When you ask what she wants, she says that she has a floral delivery for you—or for your mother or father. What do you do?

a. Ask her to put the flowers on the steps—or in the hall, if you live in an apartment. Thank her. Wait until you see her leave before opening the door.

b. Open the door and accept the flowers.

Your answer should be a. Until she leaves, *don't* open the door! This situation tests you in two ways—it challenges an idea that most people have that criminals are all men, and it

challenges your understandable desire to accept a gift. Don't assume that criminals are male and that all females (of any age or description) are "safe." You should use reasonable care and caution with *any* stranger. It's hard to resist the impulse to throw open the door and take the flowers—we've all heard that old saying about not looking a gift horse in the mouth—but you *should* resist it. The flowers will still be there in a few minutes.

If the young woman says that you have to sign for the flowers, tell her to slip the paper needing the signature through the mail chute or under the door. If after all this she doesn't leave, phone a neighbor.

It may sound like a lot of effort for a crook to buy a bouquet of flowers just to get into your home, but in one West Coast city that's just what some crooks were doing. (Of course they were stealing the flowers, not buying them.) In any case, you should not open the door in this instance.

TEST 5

Here's a situation that isn't likely to arise but helps demonstrate an important point about strangers: Your doorbell rings. You look out through the window or viewer and see a well-dressed couple who are about your parents' ages. You ask them—through the door—what you can do for them, and they answer that they are "old friends of your parents from college." They call you by name and tell you that they are in town on business and thought they'd drop by to "surprise your parents." What do you do?

>   *a.* Let them in. After all, they know your name and your
>   parents' names, and they look respectable.

b. Tell them that you're sorry but your mom is at work and your dad is asleep. Give them your mother's office telephone number and tell them to call her there. Call a parent as soon as they have gone.

If you picked *b,* you played it safe. *Don't* be caught off guard by anyone knowing your name or your parents' names or any other personal information. It is easy to get information from any number of places, such as the phone book and mailboxes, or through conversations with your neighbors. Unless *you* know them, they are strangers, and they should be treated like any other strangers.

And don't be misled by appearances. Crooks come in all shapes, sizes, and descriptions, and if crooks are going to take the time to learn your name, they are probably going to take the time to comb their hair and put on clean clothes.

TEST 6

Here's one that really tests your dedication to crime prevention: Someone knocks. You look out and see a girl about your age or even a little younger. She is crying. "Yes?" you call. "My mom's car is broken down outside," she says, "and my little brother is real sick and has to get to the doctor. Can I use your phone to call a cab?" What should you do?

    a. Let her in. She's too small to hurt you—and she needs help!

    b. Offer to make the call for her. Tell her that your dad's asleep or in the shower and that you aren't supposed to let anyone in but that you will telephone a cab for her.

    c. Tell her that your phone is out of order and direct her to a neighbor's.

Your safe answer may be either *b* or *c*. Don't let *any* stranger into your home unless you are absolutely sure the person is okay (that repairperson you've checked out, for example). In this case it may sound heartless to turn away someone in need, but if you offer to make the call, you *aren't* turning her away. And you aren't refusing to help if you direct her to a neighbor's either, especially if the neighbor is in a better position to give direct assistance. Of course, if you suspect that the stranger is a crook, you should alert your neighbor right away.

A number of similar cases occurred a couple of years ago in several small suburban areas. A pair of teenage girls knocked at doors and asked politely if they could use the bathroom. Kindhearted occupants let them in, and it wasn't until later that they found that the girls had stolen jewelry, billfolds, and other valuables on their "innocent" trip to the bathroom.

In an emergency you can be helpful and still be safe. Don't feel that any plea for help is a reason to abandon your usual safety habits.

TEST 7

Apartment dwellers have some special safety concerns. Here's a test for those of you who live in an apartment. House dwellers can take the test too—the information may come in handy someday.

Your door buzzer rings. You push the button and ask who it is. It's your neighbor and she's locked herself out of 4C (*again*). Or it's your neighbor's second cousin, who has just flown in from North Nowhere as a terrific surprise for your

neighbor. Should you buzz your neighbor in? How about your neighbor's second cousin?

a. Sure, press the buzzer. It's only neighborly. You'd expect your neighbors to do the same for you.

b. No, don't press the buzzer.

The safe answer is b. Don't buzz in your neighbor unless you are sure it *is* your neighbor. And *never* buzz a stranger into your apartment building. 4C's second cousin is a stranger to you.

It's only neighborly for apartment dwellers to work together to protect one another, and one way they do this is by keeping strangers out of their building. Police urge people to get to know their neighbors in apartment buildings, and they warn apartment dwellers to use extreme caution in buzzing *anyone* into the building.

FINAL EXAM

Someone knocks or falls against your door. You look out and see someone sprawled on your front step or in the hall outside your apartment. What do you do?

a. Open the door, leaving the chain on, to get a better look.

b. Go to the phone and call the police or an ambulance.

c. Phone a neighbor.

Your safe answers are b and c. Don't open the door, and don't trust the chain. Don't underestimate the cleverness of some crooks! Do phone the police or an ambulance, and a neighbor.

Does all of this seem paranoid or rude? Do you still feel uncomfortable about refusing to open your door? You shouldn't. No one is going to judge you badly for being careful. *Real* repair or delivery persons won't care if you are cautious. They probably wish their own kids used such good sense. Your parents' long-lost friends won't be upset if you refuse to throw open the door and invite them in. Frankly, if they are upset about your playing it safe, they probably deserve to stay lost. In any emergency—medical, car breakdown, or whatever—you can help the person who comes to your door by making the appropriate phone call *without* letting him or her in.

It's *your* house and *your* decision. Be polite, confident, and *firm* with the people who come to your door.

If you do accidentally open the door to a suspicious or frightening stranger, you can slip out through the open door and run to a neighbor's. This is the best solution and should be accompanied by a top-level power yell, unless the intruder is armed. Or you can retreat to your home's "safe room" (see page 80) and telephone the police. Or you can cooperate with the intruder. Whatever you do, you should remain absolutely calm. If you are calm, you may be able to think of a sensible solution to your problem, as did a girl who was in her apartment when burglars came in off the fire escape. The phone rang and she told the caller in French that she was being robbed. The police were called and the robbers caught.

Answering the Phone

Use the same common sense to deal with people on the phone that you use to deal with people at the door. Test your phone sense with the situations that follow.

The phone rings. You answer it and a cheerful voice says, "Hi, I'm Melvin Mumble. Is your dad in?" What do you say?

a. Say no and ask to take a message.

b. Say, "Yes, he's home, but he's busy," and ask to take a message.

c. Say that your parents are divorced and your dad doesn't live with you.

The correct answer is *b*. Don't tell anyone that you are at home alone, and never tell a stranger that you and your mom live alone. Say that your dad—or mom, if that is who the caller asked for—is busy and will return the call later. Phone your parent as soon as possible, and relay the message so that the call can be returned.

What if the caller persists? Suppose you have offered to take a message, but Melvin Mumble says, "Gosh, I really need to speak to him. Can't you just ask him if he'll be around in a half hour so that I can drop off these insurance forms?" What do you do *now?*

a. Say, "I'm sorry, but he's in the shower. I'll have him phone you later."

b. Say, "Well, he really isn't home right now, but he'll be home real soon, I think."

Here, the safe answer is *a.* Once you've started, you can't turn back without sounding silly. Don't admit that you lied, and *don't* use wishy-washy "qualifier" phrases like "I think" or "I guess" or "maybe." Say that your dad is busy—in the tub or the shower, asleep, or whatever—and say that you'll give him the message. Then hang up. You've said all you need to say.

TEST 3

Here's a more complex situation: You answer the phone. It's Miss Jackson, the counselor from your school. "I'm just updating the files," she says, "and I need to know where your mother works." What should you do?

  a. Give her the information. After all, Miss Jackson *is* your school counselor.

  b. Tell her that your mom's in the shower and you'll have her return the call. If she persists and asks you to give the information, say that you're sorry, you can't give personal information over the phone, and you'll have your mom phone her right back.

The playing-safe answer is *b*. Maybe it is Miss Jackson—and maybe it isn't. If it is, she will surely understand your sensible caution. It is really very easy for anyone to find out the name of the counselor or principal or teachers or *students* at any school. One large city has a problem every fall with kids receiving calls from "someone in the school district office" who asks the kids personal questions that start out "normally" but become obscene. A number of kids have been understandably frightened and upset by these calls.

TEST 4

Here's another situation that has occurred in several parts of the country. The company name may change, but the tactic is the same.

The phone rings and you answer it. It is a "survey representative from KidCount Data Company." The pleasant voice tells you that *you* have been chosen to take part in a national

survey of kids' attitudes toward different issues and products. You will *finally* get to tell someone what you really think of school lunches, curfew, and electronic games that eat your quarter without giving you a game in return. What an opportunity! What should you do?

> *a.* Sound off! How many chances like this are you going to get?
>
> *b.* Say that you're sorry but you're helping your dad right now. The caller will have to get someone else.

It's hard to miss out on a chance to sound off, but the safe answer is *b. Never give personal information to strangers (remember?). A criminal might use just this sort of tactic to "size up" you or your property.*

FINAL EXAM

The situation really tests your cool: The phone rings. You answer it, and no one speaks. Or someone begins to speak in an obscene manner. What should you do?

a. Power yell or blow your whistle into the phone, breaking the creep's eardrums.

b. Hang up immediately.

Your answer should be *b.* People who make obscene phone calls do it to get a response. They expect you to act shocked. Don't give them what they want! Hang up immediately without comment. If obscene or nuisance phone calls continue, report them to your telephone company's business office. Most phone companies have a department that handles this type of call—get the number from the operator—and can give you help in handling future calls.

If *any* telephone situation makes you feel threatened or flustered, it's important to remember that you can just hang up.

Your telephone sense can work even when you're not at home. Telephone answering machines are a modern convenience that can be convenient for burglars too, unless you use them with care. Some safety experts caution against answering machines and advise people to use answering services instead, but your family may prefer a machine. If you do have an answering machine, don't leave messages telling where you are or how long you'll be gone. Don't, for example, say, "Hi, this is Jimmy. My family and I will be in Florida for the next two weeks." You may as well leave the front door unlocked and tell burglars where the peanut butter is if they want to make a sandwich while they're inside. Give this type of message instead: "Hi, this is Jimmy. I'm busy right now, but if you leave your name, I'll get back to you as soon as possible."

How did you do on these sample situations? Can you think of other situations that would challenge your "safety savvy"? You don't need to be paranoid to be prepared. Planning your response to a variety of troublesome events will help you gain confidence in your ability to cope with *any* situation.

3. GETTING AROUND—
By Foot, on Public Transportation, and in Cars

"A friend of mine had his billfold stolen while he was riding on the bus, and a girl I know was hassled by some guys when she was down at the park. I want to be able to feel safe when I go out."
—ROXANNE

Your attitude and body are "tuned up" (Chapter 1), you've tested your home safety savvy (Chapter 2), and you're ready to take your skills to the streets. It's great that you're feeling confident about yourself, but before you leave, take a minute to do a final "run down."

Clothes and Equipment

• *How are you dressed?* No, this isn't a fashion quiz. Call it a "clothing consciousness" session.

Are you wearing tight pants or a tight skirt? Are you teetering atop high heels? Or do you have on comfortable, flat shoes and reasonably loose clothing? High heels and tight clothes slow you down if you want or need to run in a troublesome situation. You can't beat jeans and tennis shoes for "quick exits," but they aren't appropriate for every occasion. Think about what you're wearing and *where* you'll be going. If you're going to be walking through an unfamiliar or high-crime neighborhood or walking home after dark, you may want to think about wearing your trusty jeans and sneakers, or taking them with you to change into.

Do you have on gold neck chains or expensive (or expensive-looking) rings, watches, or earrings? Don't wear jewelry where it can be seen when you are on the street, bus, or subway or in public places such as concerts or shopping

DO   DON'T

areas. You will have to decide when extra caution is advisable. Tuck watches and bracelets inside your shirt or jacket cuffs (some kids hide them under terry cloth athletic wrist bands), leave expensive rings and earrings at home, and slip neck chains and necklaces inside shirts or sweaters. In some cities, gangs of thugs have run past bus stops, theater lines, and the like, yanking off gold neck chains as they passed. Use the same good sense about jewelry that you use about clothes. Decide what's appropriate for the occasion, and what's safe.

Are you bundled up? Hoods, hats, and umbrellas are necessary in cold or rainy weather, but they cut down on your "peripheral vision"—your ability to see objects off to the side—and hoods and hats muffle sound. This is an important *traffic* safety consideration too, so you'll want to be extra-alert when you're using an umbrella or wearing a hood or hat.

• *What are you carrying?* Are you loaded down like a pack mule? Some people can't go to the corner store without packing pajamas, a parachute, a snow tire, and a sack lunch. If that describes *you*, it's time to change your ways. The convict "experts" consulted for the videotape survey discussed in Chapter 1 often chose victims who were loaded down with packages and bulky briefcases or purses. If you carry a purse, backpack, or bookbag, dump all your stuff out. What do you *really* need? Leave unnecessary items at home.

Are you carrying cash or other valuables? While you're sorting through your things, try to "weed out" expensive items such as cameras, calculators, and electronic games *and* all excess cash. Carry only as much money as you need plus a small amount for emergencies.

Are you wired for sound? Some kids carry tape decks,

cassette players, or radios. Don't! They are especially attractive to thieves, and if you're listening to one of them (especially one with earphones), you can't hear what is going on around you. Talk about tuning out! One East Coast city has even considered a ban on earphone use by pedestrians because of the traffic safety problems. Pedestrians or bicyclists using earphones can't hear car horns, approaching sirens, or other warning signals.

If you are *really* uneasy in your own neighborhood or in a neighborhood that you must regularly walk through, you might consider using a tactic practiced by some big-city kids who live in dangerous neighborhoods. They carry a dollar or two "mugger's money" in a cheap billfold. They know that if they are ever approached by a mugger, they can turn over the billfold with little loss and little risk of further problems. This may be pretty extreme for your area, but if street robberies are a problem where you live and if you are worried about them, a couple of dollars and a castoff billfold might provide you with a little peace of mind.

• *Where do you carry your money and key?* Don't carry your key in your bag, purse, or backpack. These items all probably contain some identification. Don't label your key with your name or address. A lost key is a pain in the neck; a key lost together with your address is an invitation for a burglary. Keep your key in a front pocket, preferably one that snaps, zips, or buttons shut. If you "wear" your key on a string or chain around your neck, keep it tucked inside your shirt, blouse, or sweater so that you don't unthinkingly advertise that you let yourself in and out of the house and are at home alone at least some of the time.

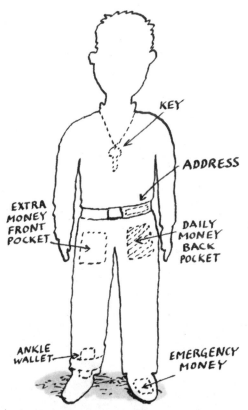

You probably have to carry some money for purchases, lunches, bus fare, and the like, and you should always carry some change as "emergency money." Put the emergency money in one place, the daily money in another. Use a front pocket, a sock, a shoe, a jogger's wrist or ankle wallet, or a wallet that hooks onto your belt. If you carry a monthly bus pass, put it into a front pocket.

Somewhere, in a billfold or inside a notebook, you should carry a list of telephone numbers including parents' work numbers, the police or "central emergency" number, the number of a trusted neighbor, and the number of your building's manager or superintendent if you live in an apartment. You should also carry an identification card giving the name and number of a person to be notified in case of an emergency.

How did you check out? Are you ready to go? Okay, close and lock the windows, lock the doors, pocket your key, and take off!

Street Wise

Street safety depends on *how* you walk as well as *where* you walk.

Of course, if you've read from the beginning of this book, you're walking confidently—balanced and centered, looking alert and purposeful. Here are a few more safety hints. You may already practice some of them without ever having thought about them. Most are just common sense.

- *What are you carrying?* If you are carrying a purse or bag, carry it close to your body, in front, with the zipper or flap toward your body. Don't let your purse dangle loosely from your fingertips or arm.
- *Watch your response if you are bumped or jostled on the street.* Don't be surly—people *do* accidentally bump one another—but don't act intimidated either. Some criminals jostle potential victims to see if they are easily frightened.

Also remember that criminals sometimes work in pairs. One will jostle the victim while the other steals the victim's billfold. If you're bumped on the street, remain calm and continue on your way.

- *Don't be drawn into conversation with strangers.* It's just bad practice. If someone asks you for directions, give a brief reply or say, "I'm sorry, I don't know," if you aren't sure or want to avoid further questions. Then walk briskly away.

  People occasionally chat to pass the time while waiting for a bus or waiting in a line. There's nothing wrong with this, and you shouldn't be frightened, but you shouldn't enter into a conversation either. Respond politely and briefly and look away or pretend interest in something else.

  If someone asks you for help, for example in a medical emergency, go to the nearest shop or business, or find the nearest police officer, and *send* help.

If someone offers to help *you*—to carry your packages or give you a ride—look very confident, stand very tall, say "No, thank you," and walk briskly away.

You don't have to be rude or scared in any of these instances. In most cases a stranger's attempt at conversation or request for (or offer of) help is perfectly sincere. Your pleasant, confident approach will not offend anyone, but it *will* discourage someone who is using casual conversation as a means of "checking out" victims.

- *Never approach a car to offer aid or directions.* Of course, you're too "street wise" to even consider getting into a car with a stranger, but you should remember to remain well away from a car when answering a question from the car's occupant. It is easy for an abductor to pull a victim into a car and speed away. You might even decide to avoid responding to people in cars at all.

- *Always try to be home before dark.* If you must come home after dark, arrange for a ride in advance, take a taxi, or walk with another person. Walking in pairs or groups is always safer than walking alone and is especially advisable at night.

- *Walk against the traffic when you are alone or in a secluded area.* This makes it difficult for anyone in a passing automobile to bother you because you will only be noticed as the car passes, and the driver will either have to back up or go around the block to talk to you.

- *Walk near the curb if you must pass empty buildings or fields or unattended parking lots.* Vagrants and criminals often hang around these areas. If you are near the curb, it would be difficult to pull you into a building, field, or other area, and you could always step into the street and signal for help if necessary.

Think about *where* you'll be walking before you leave home. You probably know most of the streets in your neighborhood pretty well. Picture them in your mind and follow these safety suggestions.

- *Walk on well-traveled streets and roads.* Try to walk where there are businesses, shops, and busy bus stops.
- *Avoid questionable areas.* Stay away from areas with spreading shrubs, vacant buildings, and unattended or poorly lit parking lots. Again, these are perfect hiding places for criminals.
- *Take the safest direct route to your destination.* Don't "cut through" fields, backyards, or alleys.
- *If you must walk home after dark, avoid dark streets.* Know *in advance* which businesses are open late and which streets are busiest, and use that information to help plan your route.
- *Insist on adequate lighting.* If the streets in your neighborhood are poorly lit, phone your city's police department and

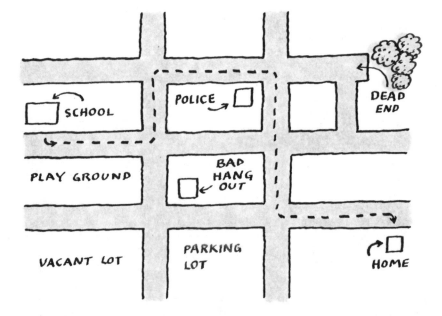

complain. See Chapter 6 for further ideas about this.

- *Vary your route occasionally.* This is a good idea if you can do it safely. It is especially important if you follow a fixed schedule and route every day. For example, try to alter the pattern somewhat if you *always* walk down Elm to Spruce and over to Alder at exactly 8:10 each morning and always walk over Alder to Spruce and up Elm at exactly 3:15 every afternoon. It's unlikely that anyone is watching you closely, but don't take a chance. If you decide to change your route and you have neighbors who watch out for you along the way, be sure to tell them of your plans.

What will you do if, despite all your careful planning, you are followed, harassed, or assaulted on the street or in any other public place? This isn't likely, especially if you regularly practice all the crime prevention habits we've discussed, but you should still think about it. Effective action in an emergency—*any* emergency, from a blown fuse to a bad burn to a personal safety emergency—requires careful advance planning. It will help your confidence if you know you have an emergency plan, and as the criminal "experts" showed in the videotape discussed in Chapter 1, increasing your confidence will help *decrease* your chances of becoming the victim of a crime. Take the time now to develop your own "action plan" to cope with troublesome situations on the street.

- *Are you being followed?* If you think that someone is following you on foot, stop, turn around, and take a look. It could be you're scared for no good reason. If you still think someone is following you, cross the street and walk back in the direction from which you just came. If the person continues to follow you, run toward the nearest busy area, home, or business and power yell for help.

- *Should you go home?* If you are walking home and think that someone is following you, do *not* go home. You should never reveal where you live to anyone you feel threatened by, and if no one will be at home when you arrive, you could be exposing yourself to danger. If you think you are being followed, go to a friend's, a school, or a business or store and ask for help.

- *Notice the traffic.* If you think that a car is circling the block and watching you, cross the street quickly or go to a busy intersection, bus stop, business, or home and ask for help.

- *If you are accosted.* If someone hollers at you or verbally harasses you in any way, don't respond. Pretend you did not hear what was said and walk quickly, purposefully, and calmly toward a busy area.

- *Dealing with muggers.* If you are approached by someone who demands your billfold, watch, or another valuable, co-operate. Don't yell, don't struggle. Remain *very* calm. A mugger will not usually hurt you unless he or she panics.

Remember, odd as it may seem, you and the mugger are in this together—and *your* job is to keep the mugger from panicking. If the mugger wants your billfold, take a deep breath and say, "I'll get it, it's in my pocket." Or if the mugger wants your watch or jacket, say, "Here, I'll take it off." Indicate cooperation. This isn't *cowardly*—you are using your good sense and your safety skills to protect yourself. Remember, no *thing* is worth your personal safety.

- *If you are grabbed by someone.* If someone tries to take you somewhere, either on foot or by car, you must use your own good judgment. Does the person have a weapon? If so, you will have to cooperate, although you should continue to look for a means of escape and try to think of verbal ways out of your situation (read the section on passive resistance in Chapter 8). If the person is not armed and there are other people around and you feel confident, you can consider using a power yell. Be prepared to follow up with a quick escape and a full-speed run. In any situation like this, you must always think two or three steps ahead, and you should never start anything—an excuse, a yell, or any other resistance—unless you are committed to it. Some programs, especially some rape prevention programs, teach physical resistance skills. You should use these *only* if you have had thorough training in using them and are confident of your skills.

Public Transportation

If you ride buses, trains, or subways, you have other opportunities to add to your store of safety skills. Here are a few general rules that apply to all forms of public transportation.

• *Know where you're going in advance.* Consult a transit map, a transit company information office, or a knowledgeable adult. Know which bus, train, or subway to take—and where to catch it and exactly where to get off. Know, too, which bus, train, or subway to take home and where to catch *it.* Write this information down so that you can consult it later if you get confused.

• *Wait at busy, well-lit stops.* If possible, try to avoid isolated stops and stations. In off-peak hours, stand near the token booth until the train arrives.

• *Have your pass ready.* Have your bus pass or exact change ready in a front pocket as you approach the stop or station. Don't sift through a big wad of money looking for the correct change.

• *Stand back from the subway or train platform.*

• *Choose a safe seat.* Try to sit up front near the driver on a bus or in a well-occupied car in a subway or train. In a subway, try to sit in the same car as the conductor. Avoid the rear car.

• *Traveling in a crowd.* If you are standing in a crowd of people, be conscious of your wallet or purse. Keep your purse close to your body; put your wallet in a front pocket. Don't put your billfold in a back pocket—it's too easy to steal it without your notice.

- *Watch your belongings.* When you are seated, keep your bags, backpack, or purse in your lap with your arms *firmly* around them. If you are seated near the window, wedge your purse between your body and the wall of the bus or train. Be especially careful of your belongings if you are seated near an exit. In some cities, crooks grab a bag or purse from a passenger's lap, run out the exit door, and get lost in the crowd.
- *Remain alert when you are traveling.* The motion of a moving vehicle is sometimes relaxing, and if you're seated and have had a busy day, it's easy to get drowsy—or even to go to sleep! Keep yourself awake and aware of what's going on.
- *If someone on the bus or subway is bothering you.* If this happens, move closer to the driver or conductor.
- *When you reach your stop.* When you get off the bus, subway, or train, walk briskly and purposefully away.

Cars

Automobile passengers have their own set of safety rules to follow. A passenger is often able to help the driver by serving as a second set of eyes and ears when the driver is busy with red lights, traffic jams, and parking problems. Here are some "rules of the road" to help you protect yourself and the people with whom you ride.

- *Don't accept a ride with anyone you don't know.* Hitchhiking is dangerous—don't do it. It puts your own safety out of your control. Hitchhiking isn't the only instance in which you might be tempted to accept a ride with a stranger, though. What if your very best friend Mary offers you a ride home with *her* friend Becky's older brother Dave? If you—and your family—don't know Becky *and* Dave, don't take the ride. Nice people can have creepy relatives, and even nice relatives can be *awful* drivers.

- *Look over the interior of any car before you get in.* The chances of anyone lurking inside are very remote, especially if the car has been locked, but experts still recommend a quick "once over." It's even advisable to look *under* the car as you approach it. In some areas, criminals hide under cars and can grab a driver's ankles as he or she enters the car, throwing the driver off balance.

- *Lock the car door as soon as you get in.* And keep it locked until you arrive at your destination.

- *Keep the windows rolled up.* It's safest to avoid traveling through high-crime areas at all. Whenever possible, select an alternate route. If you must ride through a bad neighborhood, however, keep the car windows rolled up.

- *Don't display valuables or packages inside the car.* Stow them in the trunk or place them on the floor of the car. Don't leave packages in the car when you get out; lock them safely in the trunk.

- *If you see someone in trouble.* Police advise drivers *not* to stop if they see an accident or another car in distress. Police say that it is safer for the driver to continue to the next public telephone and call for professional help. This advice may be inappropriate if you live in a community where people *always* stop to help one another out. As with any crime prevention tip, you need to know what is appropriate and safe in *your* area.

- *If you are in trouble.* Police also warn drivers not to stop immediately if another driver signals that something is wrong with *your* car or even if your car is bumped by another car. If possible, drivers should stop only at well-lit, public areas such as service stations or attended parking lots.

- *If your car breaks down away from town.* Police recommend the following:

    Tie a "flag"—a scarf, a sock or something similar—to the radio antenna. If your car has no antenna, tie your flag to the side-view mirror.

    Raise the car's hood.

    Get back into the car. Roll up the windows, lock the doors, flip on the car's hazard light, and honk the horn.

When someone does stop, ask him or her to telephone the police or a towing service and send help.

- *Whenever possible, use parking lots that are attended and well-lit.* Remain especially alert when in a parking lot. *Any* parking lot poses safety problems.

- *Multilevel parking.* If you must use a parking structure with an elevator to parking "levels," you should read the elevator safety tips on page 48.

- *If your car is being followed.* If you or anyone else in your car think that you are being followed by another car, experts say *don't go home!* Drive toward the closest busy area, blinking car lights and honking the horn. By doing this, one woman led her pursuer right to the local police station!

- *Be alert when you get out of the car after arriving home.* This is especially important at night. If your porch or garage lights aren't on timers (see Chapter 6), leave the car lights on until you can flip on a porch or garage light.

- *When you leave the car.* Roll up the car windows, lock the car doors, and remove the car keys *whenever* you leave the car. People sometimes get lazy when they are only going to be out of the car "for a minute," but it only takes "a minute" for a thief to clean out a car and be gone. Or to steal the car and be *long* gone.

Cars, trains, subways, buses, and your own trusty two feet can take you where you need to go. Your own good sense and crime prevention concern can see that you get there safely and can guide you toward appropriate responses in all situations.

4. PUBLIC POLICY—
Uptown, Downtown,
and All Around
the Town

"I don't want to get ripped off when I'm shopping or at school. I babysit a lot, too. Are there special job safety tips?"
—SARAH

Y ou've followed all the hints in Chapter 3 and now you're *there*—wherever it was that you were going. Now what?

Use the same sensible skills you've been using all along to stay safe in all public places and situations.

Shopping Centers, Stores, and Malls

Kids shop out of necessity—they buy lettuce and lightbulbs and shampoo. And they shop for fun—they buy clothes, records or tapes, and games. And they eat in restaurants and go to movies and skating rinks, and they go to stores to play electronic games. All these shopping situations are covered by the following "public policies":

- *Stay in busy areas.* Avoid little-used entrances and parking lots. Parking lots pose great safety problems. If you must use one, see safety tips in Chapter 3.

- *Don't flash your cash.* Carry only what you will need, and don't display any more money than you require for each purchase. Suppose you are going over to the mall to buy a record and to meet a friend for lunch. How much will the record cost? Put *that* amount in your right front pocket. How much will lunch cost? You can probably make a good estimate. Put *that* amount in your left front pocket. Now, when you pay for the record, you won't have to pull out a big wad of cash *or* get a big bill back in change. Thieves sometimes stand near cash registers and watch customers, then follow them out of the store.

- *Watch out for your belongings.* Remain aware of your purse, bag, or backpack whenever you are out in public. Don't set them down even for "just a minute." If you need to free your hands, keep your pack on your back and tuck your bag or purse under your arm. Or have a friend hold your things. Be careful with your purse or pack in dressing rooms too. Don't leave them behind while you step out to grab another shirt, and watch them closely in big, crowded "group" dressing rooms.

- *Avoid public restrooms.* When possible, avoid restrooms that are open to easy public traffic. They are occasionally used as hangouts by criminals. It's safer to use restrooms in restaurants and department stores.

- *Think before you talk.* Don't discuss private matters in public places. You can't be sure *who* is listening as you tell Jill about your vacation plans, your babysitting job for Saturday night, or your family's great new stereo.

- *Try not to buy too many things on a single trip.* Don't be loaded down with sacks and shopping bags on your return home (see suggestions in the Clothes and Equipment section of Chapter 3). Remember the videotape study discussed in Chapter 1? Criminals often choose people burdened with packages as potential victims.

Elevators

Many buildings have self-service elevators, and so you will probably have lots of occasions to use these elevator safety hints.

- *Don't ride in a self-service elevator with anyone who makes you uncomfortable.* Remember, you have to trust your instincts. If you are waiting for an elevator with someone—a man *or* a woman—who makes you uneasy, let the person get on the elevator first and then walk away.

    "Oh, no, how embarrassing!" you may think. After all, he or she could be a perfectly nice person. Yes, most people *are* perfectly nice, but that is no reason for you to put yourself in an uncomfortable situation, especially not when you can so easily remove yourself from it. Trust your instincts!

    If you're still worried about hurting someone's feelings by walking away, try this: As soon as the other person gets on the elevator, and *before* you get on (strangers first is always a good policy), clap your hand to your forehead or snap your fingers as though you've just remembered something. Walk briskly away.

    This routine also works if you're waiting for the elevator, and when it stops at your floor, there is already someone in there who makes you uncomfortable. It even works if a suspicious stranger gets on after you!

- *Plan your elevator strategy.* If, despite all these hints, you find yourself alone in an elevator with a stranger who worries you, stand near the control panel. Push the button for the next available floor. If the other person bothers you *in any way* between floors, push the elevator alarm button. If the other person follows you off the elevator, especially if you get off at a floor other than the one that the other person pushed, start power yelling for help *immediately!*

- *Use the same good sense on stairwells.* If you think that someone is following you, enter the next hallway, and if the other person follows you, yell for help.

Parks

Parks are popular play spaces for most kids. Unfortunately, they are sometimes popular hangouts for criminals too. You

can still visit and enjoy your community parks, but play it safe. Follow these suggestions.

- Don't take money with you to the park except for emergency money and whatever small change you will need for refreshments or transportation.
- Try to avoid public restrooms in parks.
- Stay in busy areas. Don't wander off to secluded sections of the park.
- Visit the park with your friends, rather than alone. It's more fun and much safer!
- Don't take your bike to the park if you will have to leave it unattended unless there is a bike rack, or a place near the play area where you can lock your bike. See Chapter 7 for bicycle safety tips.

Schools

Use the same common sense at school as you use in every other public place.

- *Keep an eye on your belongings.* Watch your pack or purse. Try to avoid taking valuable items to school, but if you must, leave them with a teacher or in the school office for safekeeping.
- *Your school locker is your "home away from home."* You need to be as security conscious about your locker as you are about your house or apartment. If you have a combination lock, *don't* tell the combination to anyone, not even your friends. Suppose your friends tell it to their friends, who tell

it to *their* friends, and so on until, one day, you find that you are sharing a locker with a cast of thousands, and your "home away from home" is about as secure as a pup tent on a subway platform.

- *If you use a padlock on your school locker.* Buy a sturdy lock and keep the key in a front pocket with your house key. Most padlocks come with two keys; keep the spare key in a safe place at home.

- *Watch your belongings carefully in the gym locker room.* If you must remove watches or other jewelry, lock them up in your teacher's office, if possible.

- *If you are in school before or after normal school hours.* If you have to be in school during off-hours for sports or music practice or whatever, try to avoid isolated areas.

- *Always report suspicious characters.* If you see suspicious characters either in or outside school, report them to a teacher or to the office.

Jobs

If you have a job or are thinking about getting one, there are some safety considerations to keep in mind.

- *Reading the ads.* Be suspicious of advertisements—classified or poster ads—offering jobs with high wages and bonus "prizes" for kids. A few ads like this are legitimate, for example ads for paper routes. Some are frauds, for instance selling door-to-door for some very questionable companies that exploit cheap labor. And a few are "traps" set to lure kids. If you see an ad that interests you, have an adult call on your behalf. If the job seems legitimate, then you can call. Some jobs can be checked out through the Chamber of Commerce or Better Business Bureau in your community.
- *Job interviews.* Don't agree to meet anyone at his or her home for a job interview unless it is a "home-based" job such as child care or yardwork. For a business-based job, you should be given an interview at the place of business during regular business hours.
- *Telephone job offers.* If you are telephoned by a stranger about doing yardwork or babysitting or a similar job, ask the caller who recommended you for the job, then tell the caller that you have to check with a parent and will phone back. Call the person who recommended you for the job. If that checks out, ask a parent for an opinion and then phone the caller back and say that you would like to stop by on Saturday (or whenever) for a few minutes to meet the children

you'll be caring for, or to size up the lawn you'll be mowing, or just to discuss the job further. Agree upon a time for this preliminary meeting, and have a parent or other adult drive you and wait in the car while you are inside.

This may seem like a lot of bother to you, but it makes good sense. If, at the preliminary meeting, *anything* about the person, house, or situation makes you *at all* uneasy, refuse the job. You can either turn down the job on the spot, or if you'd be more comfortable, say that you need to discuss the offer with a parent and will call later. Phone the person when you get home and refuse the job. It's important to really listen to your instincts in this situation. You are not going to earn enough money to make it worthwhile to take risks!

- *Child-care jobs.* If you will be caring for a child, especially at night, you should explain your interest in personal safety and crime prevention and ask about locks (see Chapter 6 for suggestions on lock safety). Don't be timid—be safe. Parents will probably be (and should be) pleased that you're so mature and responsible. After all, it's also their child's safety you're looking after. If you are very uneasy about the house's locks or other safety features, don't take the job.

- *How will you get to and from your job?* Does it require you to walk or to ride on public transportation after dark? Is it worth the risk? Can you arrange for a parent to provide transportation, or can you walk home with another worker?

- *How safe is the neighborhood where you'll be working?* Most police departments can give you this information. If the neighborhood has a high crime rate, you'll have to decide if you should take special precautions or refuse the job.

- *Practice safety on the job.* If you are caring for a child, use some of the skills you learned in Chapter 2. Ask the parent for—and write down—the telephone numbers of two *trusted* neighbors. Get exact names and exact numbers, not just "Mrs. Jones across the street." And don't forget to ask for the telephone number where the parent can be reached in an emergency. While you are on the job, be especially careful of telephone callers or of persons at the door. Say that "Mr. Smith is in the shower and can't come to the door" or that "Ms. Wilson is ill. Can she phone you later?" Don't let anyone in while you are alone, and never let anyone know that you are alone.

Social Situations

You probably enjoy visiting your friends and going places with them, or going on dates. You are usually perfectly safe in these situations. However, here are a few instances that deserve special attention.

- *You know that you should never accept rides with strangers.* And strangers include even your best friend Mary's friend Becky's brother Dave (see Chapter 3). But what if it isn't a ride that Dave offers, but an invitation to a party? Suppose that Mary's friend Becky's brother Dave (busy guy, Dave) is having a humongous party Saturday night with an all-you-can-eat pizza buffet, a live rock band, door prizes, and a raffle for a trip to Disneyland. How can you refuse a deal like that? Easily. Think about the ten thousand high school kids who will hear about it and be drawn to it like ants to a pic-

nic. Then figure out how much pizza—or fun—you'll really have. If you and your family don't know and feel comfortable about someone, *don't* go to his or her house. If you want to check out a new friend, invite him or her to your house first. And be sure that the invitation is for a time when a parent is at home.

- *Use the same good sense about dates.* Don't accept "blind dates" except for very controlled situations—like a Sunday dinner with your family. It's an unfortunate fact that almost *one third* of all rapes are committed by someone known to the victim, and "date rapes" are not uncommon. Don't become a statistic. Refuse blind dates unless you can check the person out thoroughly with *trusted* friends *and* unless the dating situation is very controlled and public. You should keep all dates public, even those with someone you know, until you are very sure that you can trust the person.

It's probably harder to hear your instincts signaling in social situations than it is at other times. Promises of a good time and popularity often drown out that nagging voice that tells you to "watch out, be careful." But you *can* do both—have a good time *and* be careful. Just use reasonable caution in all situations and make social choices that put *you* and your safety first.

Once you are sure of your safety skills—at home and away—it's time to spread the word and enlist the help of neighbors, friends, and family members in your crime prevention efforts.

5. NOSY NEIGHBORS— A Protection Partnership

"There have been a lot of muggings in my neigh-borhood lately. I mean, it's like taking your life in your hands to walk to the bus stop. It really makes me mad. I'd like to see the neighbors get together and turn things around." —LIN

Street and home safety starts with all the people who live and work in your neighborhood. Through its interest, or lack of interest, in crime prevention your neighborhood sends "signals" to would-be criminals in just the same way that you send signals through your attitude and bearing. What signals is *your* neighborhood sending?

Does your neighborhood participate in a Block Home, Helping Hand, Crimewatch, or Whistlestop program? These are all names for programs in which neighbors work together to protect one another from crime. The programs are very effective. Some big-city neighborhoods have cut burglary rates in *half* by starting a watch program and using simple security measures.

Participants in neighborhood programs usually display window stickers so that passersby—and potential troublemakers—know that the neighborhood works together to keep its citizens safe. If you see these stickers in your neighborhood, find out how you can get involved.

Discuss your interest with your family (see Chapter 6 for suggestions on starting a family crime prevention discussion). If your family is too busy to participate, *you* can still get involved. In many families, kids are actually at home and in the neighborhood more than their parents, and it might be that your Crimewatch group is made up of senior citizens, neighborhood shopkeepers, and concerned kids like you. The ages of the participants are not important; all that is important is that they share a commitment to crime prevention.

If your family approves of your intention to get involved, find out who the crime prevention coordinator is in your neighborhood by asking a neighbor or phoning the police. With this type of call, do *not* use the police emergency number. Look in the phone book for the appropriate number, either a general nonemergency number or a special "crime prevention" number.

If your neighborhood isn't involved in a watch program, talk to the neighbors and find out why not. Tell them about the benefits of such a program—the police department can often supply you with convincing pamphlets. Talk to other kids, to adult friends, to youth group or church leaders, and to teachers if you attend school in your neighborhood or know the teachers at the school in your neighborhood. If your neighborhood

or area has a community organization, talk to the organization's leaders about holding a crime prevention meeting. The police will sometimes send speakers to these meetings to talk about community crime prevention and help organize watch groups. You have to request speakers well in advance of your meeting.

If the police department in your area doesn't have a speakers bureau or if a speaker isn't available, *you* can speak, using pamphlets or information from the police department. You might also get the name of a community organizer from a neighborhood that *does* have a watch program and ask him or her to speak to your neighborhood group.

What if your neighborhood or community doesn't have an organization? How can you reach people to get them involved in a watch program?

If you are in Scouts or a similar program, get your club or

organization interested in forming a watch program as a special project. You can also talk to the officials at area churches, community centers, senior citizen centers, school parents' groups, and to the owners of businesses in your area. Be sure to take supporting information with you when you talk to people. Pamphlets work well because you can leave them behind and give people something to think about. Follow up your visits with a "friendly reminder" phone call.

The easiest thing in the world for people to do is nothing at all. You may have to push and pester your neighbors into action, but your efforts will pay off in reduced crime—*and* reduced concern about crime.

What can you and your neighbors do to protect yourselves and one another?

- *Form a "protection partnership."* Agree to keep an eye and ear on one another's houses and apartments, and promise to report anything suspicious to police.

- *Keep shrubs and trees trimmed and entrances well lit at night.* See Chapter 6 for more ideas. Make sure that you *can* watch one another's homes.

- *Know the neighborhood "schedules."* Exchange schedules with your closest and most trusted neighbors—or with the ones who are at home the most. If Mr. Hill across the street *knows* that you are at school from 8 A.M. to 3 P.M. and knows that you *always* leave the cat inside and the front door closed and locked, he will know that something is wrong if your cat is smelling the roses in the front yard at noon and your front door is wide open. Discuss routines with your neighbors when you swap schedules. *How* do you get to school? Do you ride the bus, does a parent drive you, or do you walk? Do you walk alone, with other neighborhood kids, or do you *usually* walk with six tall, masked men? It's important for your neighbors to understand what's normal so that they can report anything abnormal. Be sure to tell neighbors when your schedule or routine changes so that you don't set off a false alarm!

- *Neighbors can be especially helpful at vacation times.* Safety experts say that it is a good idea to tell all your trusted neighbors when you're leaving on a trip. A spare key and special instructions should be left with one neighbor, who can come in every day and raise and lower shades and curtains as you would have them if you were at home; bring in the milk, mail, and paper; and water outside plants. Any deliveries should be stopped if you're going to be gone for more than a few days. Offer to line up one of your trusted

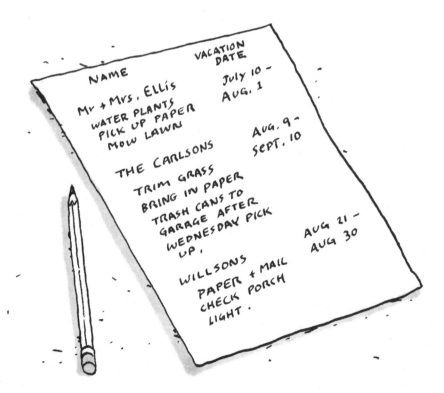

friends to do some yardwork while your family is away. The grass should be kept clipped in the spring and summer, the leaves should be raked in the fall and the snow shoveled in winter. It's a dead giveaway that you're gone if there's three feet of untracked snow in front of your house.

- *Get everyone involved.* Neighbors help one another, too, when they all practice personal, home, and property safety. Word goes out on the criminal "grapevine" that some neighborhoods are more secure than others. Criminals naturally gravitate toward easier targets.

- *Businesses are part of many neighborhoods.* Business owners and employees should be included in any watch programs.

- *Community Crimewatch programs are just as important if you live in the country.* It may even be easier to organize country neighbors, who are more likely to know one another and may be used to helping one another in other ways. Country neighbors can watch for strange cars. They should also exchange schedules (especially vacation schedules!), display Crimewatch stickers, and start a "phone pal" program to protect isolated, especially elderly, neighbors. Ask the police in the nearest town, or the country sheriff, for crime tips for rural dwellers.

Many neighborhoods have gone beyond watch programs. If you are successful with your watch efforts, you might want to think about these ideas from neighbors who have found that "nosy neighbors" are the *best* insurance against crime.

- *Apartment buzzers.* Some apartment dwellers have had "buddy buzzers" installed in their apartments. A buddy buzzer is a burglar alarm that rings in the apartments on

either side of you. When the buddy buzzer goes off, neighbors phone the police.

- *Escort services.* Some places have started "escort services" to accompany senior citizens or kids or anyone traveling after dark through high-crime areas.
- *Citizen patrols.* Some neighborhood groups have organized "citizen patrols." Neighbors work in pairs, on foot or in cars, looking for suspicious strangers or unusual activity. They don't carry weapons or confront possible criminals. Instead they often carry walkie-talkies, or if they're in cars, they have CB radios so that they can quickly call for help if they see something that doesn't look "right."
- *Apartment patrols.* Apartment dwellers in some cities use smaller versions of "block patrols" to keep their building's hallways, lobbies, laundry rooms, elevators, and stairways safe.

These efforts have resulted in lower crime rates in many neighborhoods. If your neighborhood or community group is interested in any of these ideas, ask the police in your area for tips.

Foot patrolling and night escorting are best left to adults, but there is still plenty you can do to participate in your neighborhood's crime-fighting effort.

Sticker Up

Keep the police department's emergency number or your city's central emergency number *on* your phone. Encourage all your neighbors to do the same. Get these stickers from the police, or if they don't have them, make your own stickers with adhesive labels and felt-tip pens. Pass them out to your neighbors. It may seem silly to paste a number most people already know on the phone, but you'd be amazed at how many people forget the number—even a simple three-digit number—in the pressure of a real emergency.

Be a Buddy

There really is safety in numbers! Walk with other kids to school, the store, or the park. Offer to accompany younger kids too.

Become a "Phone Pal"

Check on an elderly neighbor each afternoon. Your daily call will cheer up your phone pal, and you will both be safer.

Get Involved

Report anything suspicious to the police or tell a responsible adult immediately. Keep an eye on neighbors' homes when you are at home, watch for unfamiliar cars or persons on the street, and check out unusual noises. If more people would get involved in community crime prevention, crime rates would drop in *all* neighborhoods.

Speak Up for Safety

You are gaining a lot of useful information about the attitudes and habits that help prevent crime. Share that information with younger children, classmates, and club members—with anyone who will listen to you. *Everyone* benefits when safety consciousness is raised.

Keep up the good work. Don't let your neighborhood get lazy. Keep neighbors informed, communication open, and interest high in *your* safe neighborhood.

6. HOME SAFE AGAIN—
Landscaping,
Lighting,
Locks, and More

"Our neighbors were robbed last month. Someone broke into their house and stole their stereo, television, and cameras. The next week, my folks had the police come and inspect our house. They gave us a list of security improvements we should make, starting with a new lock on the front door."
—JACKIE

You started this book at home, working on the habits and attitudes that took you safely from your home to the street and into the world beyond your neighborhood. You've worked your way back and are now, once again, "home safe." Or are you?

Safe Entrances

First, you have to get in the door. Have your key in your hand as you near your home and look around—be alert! How does your street look? Are there any strange cars or unfamiliar persons on your block? What are they doing? Are your neighbors at home? How do *their* houses or apartment buildings look?

- *If you live in a house,* give it a quick look before going in. If anything looks unusual or suspicious, go to a neighbor's and phone home first. After all, a parent or brother or sister may have come home and raised the blinds or opened the window. If there's no answer at home, phone a parent at work. *Never* go into your home if you have reason to think that someone has broken in!

- *If you live in an apartment,* look over the entrance area as you approach the building. This is especially important if your building doesn't have a doorman. If you see suspicious strangers hanging around the entrance, watch from a distance for a few minutes, and if the strangers don't go away, go to a phone and call the building manager or superintendent. Keep your manager or superintendent's number in your wallet or notebook. You should not go into your apartment if your front door is ajar or if anything looks suspicious. Go to a neighbor's and phone home. If there's no answer, phone a parent at work.

Family Involvement

Complete home security requires more than *your* "safety savvy." It requires a commitment to crime prevention by all members of your family.

You will need adult help to carry out some of the suggestions in this chapter. If you have not already done so, you should discuss your crime prevention interest with your family. Sometimes it's difficult for families to talk about crime prevention. Parents don't want to scare their kids, and many hope that if they ignore crime, it will just creep quietly away. Unfortunately, it doesn't work that way. Ignoring crime only keeps people from taking positive action to combat crime.

Find a relaxed opportunity to bring up the subject with your family—after dinner or on a lazy Sunday, maybe—and use this book to "ease into" the topic. It will help if you read the rest of the book first and make a list of specific subjects or concerns that you have about your home's security or your family's safety habits.

If you are unable to get adult help with your crime prevention effort—if the adults in your household are too busy or too uncomfortable to discuss it with you—try to get the support of

brothers or sisters, and make sure that *you* do everything that you can to make your home secure. Your parent may not want to clip the hedge, but he or she may not mind if you clip it. And remember, you don't need adult help to lock doors, use available lights wisely, and put away bicycles, lawnmowers, and other outdoor equipment.

The general home safety hints given here are good guidelines for anyone anywhere, but every home in every town doesn't need two dead-bolt locks, street-level window grates, and a burglar alarm. Yet these may be sensible precautions in a neighborhood with a high crime rate. You should tailor the crime prevention tips in this chapter to fit your community, neighborhood, and needs.

An Outside Chance

You've already learned that home safety often begins *outside* the home—in the neighborhood or community. Home safety is also affected by the exterior of your house or apartment, the opportunities it provides for "easy" crime, and the signals it sends to would-be criminals. Don't give crooks an "outside chance" at your home.

- *Garage doors.* If your house has a garage, make sure that it has a good lock, and use the lock regularly. Tools and bikes can be stolen from unlocked garages; an intruder can wait inside a garage for someone to come home; or if there is an entrance to the house through the garage, a burglar can use the shelter of the garage to have a leisurely crack at the back door lock.

- *Hidden hazards.* Does your family hide a spare key outside your house or apartment? Don't! You might think that no one would *ever* look in the hanging planter or behind the loose brick in the wall, but police warn that the "cleverest" hiding places are often the ones that crooks check first.

If you are afraid of being locked out, leave a key with a neighbor or with your apartment building's superintendent or manager.

Some people hide a key in their *neighbor's* hanging planter, but this isn't necessarily safe either. If someone finds the key during the day when most of the people are at school or work, he or she may have time to try to fit the key to the locks of several homes.

- *Free rides.* Are bicycles, lawnmowers, and other items left outside your home? A bicycle or a piece of yard equipment or lawn furniture can be stolen in a flash. Lawn furniture, stepladders, and stools can be used to climb through windows. And tools—hammer, shovels, and the like—can be used to break locks and windows. Put bikes away or lock them securely (see Chapter 7 for ideas), and lock all tools and furniture in a garage or toolshed when they are not in use.

If you live in an "open-design" apartment complex, *all* tenants need to become property conscious. Make sure that a crook doesn't use *your* lawn chair to reach your *neighbor's* window!

- *Fence sense.* Does your yard have a *very* tall fence around it or a decorative latticework screen near the doorway? Both are intended to provide privacy, and they do their job well—they provide plenty of privacy for residents, guests, *and* crooks. Police say it is safer if neighbors and passersby can see your entranceways and windows.

- *Lighten up.* Does your home have outdoor lights near

doors? Does it have yard lighting? Is your neighborhood well lit at night? Adequate outdoor and street lights discourage burglars and muggers. Here are some lighting suggestions.

Keep your entrances well lit at night if you are away. This allows neighbors to watch your home and will help you get in quickly and safely when you return.

Don't leave lights on all day if you will return home after dark. Encourage your family to put lights on timing devices, which turn the lights on at a set time, or use photoelectric cells, which come on automatically at dusk.

If you live in an apartment building, you have a right to expect lobbies, stairwells, hallways, and laundry areas to be well lit. If they are not, you should complain or ask the adults in your household to complain. If your landlord, building owner, or manager doesn't respond to your complaints, there are tenant action groups and tenant "unions" in many cities that help with problems of this type.

If you live in an open-design apartment complex, parking lots, walkways, and laundry rooms should all have adequate lighting.

Lobby for good streetlighting! The installation of improved streetlights cut crime in one Washington, D.C., neighborhood by 30 percent! Find out the name of the person to call or write in *your* city if streetlighting is inadequate.

- *Crime cutbacks.* Overgrown shrubs, trees, and hedges are the burglar's buddies. They prevent neighbors from seeing your house, and they give a crook all the time in the world to work on locks, doors, and windows. Spreading shrubs and trees with trailing limbs also provide cover for muggers. Tree limbs that are allowed to grow too near windows can give a burglar a "boost up," and overgrown limbs and branches can sometimes block street and yard lights. Chop, mow, lop, and cut. Keep your yard neat *and* safe!
- *Giveaways.* Your home, like your body and attitude, sends signals to would-be criminals. Take a good look at *your* house or apartment. What is it saying? How can you monitor its messages?

Do you live alone with your mother? Tell her that police advise against putting her name alone—Mary Smith—in the phone book or on the mailbox because some criminals think that women are easy targets for crime. Police say it's safer to use initials: M. K. Smith. Your mother might even want to use her initials and your initials: M. K. and J. J. Smith.

Do the paper, mail, and milk sit out on your front porch all day, or in the hall outside your apartment? These are all signals that no one is home. If you can't have the paper and milk delivered at a time when someone is at home to bring them in, or can't arrange for a neighbor to take them in, it's safer to cancel home delivery and pick up the paper and milk at the store. You can ask a neighbor to pick up your mail, or your family may want to think about having a mail chute installed in place of a mailbox.

Don't leave indoor lights on if you will be gone on a sunny day and don't leave outdoor lights on during the day (see Lighten Up section). Lights left on at inappropriate times tell the burglar that no one is home to turn them off.

If your home has Venetian blinds, tilt them up. That way, passersby will only be able to see your ceiling. When you leave the house, put curtains and shades in the position they are most often in when you are at home.

Encourage your family to arrange with a neighbor to watch one another's homes during vacation time.

You might think about leaving a radio on when you are away so that your home even *sounds* busy and occupied. Police recommend putting a radio on a timing device when you go away on a trip. An inexpensive timing device will turn your radio or lights on and off at set intervals, just as you would do if you were at home.

The idea is to make your home look and sound "lived in" at all times. Household burglars do not want difficulties or confrontations. If you make their job hard by reducing their "outside chance" and by making them think that someone is inside, they will leave your house alone and find an easier target.

The Ins and Outs of Doors, Locks, and Windows

At this point, it will help if you try to "think like a criminal" and take a "crook's tour" of your house or apartment. Look for the following safety problems:

• *Are doors unlocked or windows open or unlocked?* Forced entries account for fewer than one half of all home burglaries. That means that more than half the time, burglars walk in the door or climb through an unlocked window—*or* they are let in by occupants.

Are door locks weak—easy to break or pry open? Many homes and apartments have a key-in-the-knob lock. The lock has a tapered spring-operated bolt that goes from the door into the doorjamb. The lock looks like this:

This lock is easily smashed with a pipe wrench, hammer, rock, or other heavy object, and the bolt can be quickly pried open with a credit card or knife. It is usually safest to have this type of lock replaced. Read on for replacement suggestions.

Do you depend on a door chain to keep intruders out? Most security chains are worthless. They are usually so weak they can be easily snapped with a shoulder blow, *or* they have been installed with short screws that pop right out with a good shove, *or* they have so much slack in them that an intruder can stick a hand in and unfasten the chain.

Are outside doors flimsy? The best lock in the world can't protect a weak door. Look at your home's doors.

Are they "hollow core" doors? Knock on them; do they *sound* hollow? Hollow-core doors can be kicked in or sawed through by a determined burglar. If crime isn't a serious problem in your area, and if neighbors look out and listen for one another, you probably don't need to worry. But, in areas of high crime, hollow-core doors pose real safety problems.

Do your doors have set-in decorative panels of glass or wood? As with the hollow-core doors, your door may be fine for your neighborhood, but if you live in a place with a lot of home burglaries, you might consider reinforcing decorative insets with plywood or covering door glass with grillework (see page 78).

- *Can you see out* before *opening the door?* If there are no windows near your door, it's a good idea to have a "peep-hole viewer" in your door.

- *Does your door open* out *instead of* in? It's easy for a burglar to remove the entire door if the hinges and pins are on the outside.

- *How are your doorframes?* Is there a crack between the door and the frame on the lock side? If so, someone could force a crowbar into it.

  Is the frame old—the wood cracked, dried out, or rotten? Could it be splintered easily?

- *Are your windows wide open or unlocked?* Window locks are often flimsy, but they should be used anyway. If you have a window open for fresh air, fasten it with a "safety pin" (see page 78).

- *Are basement windows unscreened?* Basement windows can be broken or even removed. They should have screens, bars, or grilles for protection.

- *What other "entrances" are there?* Can your apartment be entered through a fire escape, a neighboring building, an airshaft, or an over-the-door transom? It won't help to lock your doors if you allow burglars another way in.

Take a hard look at your home. *Think like a crook.* How would *you* break in?

Once you've identified your home's "trouble spots," set to work correcting them. Here's how:

• *Lock up!* Remember, over one half of all burglaries are accomplished without force. Lock up when you leave, and lock up when you're at home. *Don't* leave a door unlocked for a parent, brother, or sister. Family members should knock or use their key.

Encourage the adults in your household to have good locks installed. If they are interested in increasing your home's security, but don't know what kind of locks to have installed, tell them that many police departments and most locksmiths can give them good advice. A single-cylinder dead-bolt lock with a bolt at least one inch long is recommended for most circumstances, although some crime prevention experts recommend *two* dead-bolts on each outside door, placed one to five feet apart on the door. The police can usually say what is recommended for your area. When locks are replaced, remind adults to check (or have checked) the "strike plate," the area into which the lock bolt fits. Be sure that you and all family members know how to open locked doors quickly in case of fire.

- *Check your doors.* It is possible to reinforce thin plywood decorative panels and put security grates or grilles over glass panels, or to replace the glass with unbreakable plastic panels. If your door is really a disaster and home burglary rates are high in your area, your family may want to replace the door.

- *Change your chain.* If you are more comfortable having a door chain or if your family prefers to have one, try to use one with strong, welded links. The chain anchor should be installed into good strong wood and attached with two-inch screws. The chain itself should only allow the door to be opened one to two inches.

- *Safeguard patio doors.* Sliding glass doors can be "locked" by putting a small section of broom handle in the door's "track" after the door is closed.

- *Lock your windows!* There are a number of ways to provide effective back-up protection for your window sash.

    Put in "safety pins." This is something that any handy adult can do while you read the instructions aloud to them. With the window closed, drill a downward slanting hole through the top corner of the lower window sash. Continue to drill halfway into the bottom corner of the upper window sash. Use nails or pins ("safety pins") to lock the window. You can even have holes drilled at different heights so that the window can be opened wider on hot days and still be "locked."

    Check air conditioners and fans. Does your family use

window air conditioners or fans? Are they locked into place—or can they be lifted out, allowing a thief to walk off with them or to come inside through the open window? Conditioners and fans should be secured with bolts. If they aren't, bring the problem to an adult's attention.

Screens, grates, and grilles help. Decorative sheet metal, iron bars, and grilles can all be used over high-risk windows and are fairly easy to install. Fire officials warn that immovable grates or grilles shouldn't be placed over fire safety exits. There are specially constructed grilles that can be pushed out in case of fire. They usually use a key or pin to unfasten them. If your family uses this kind, everyone should know how to open the grille, and the key or pin should be stored close to the window. This type of grate

should probably not be used in a small child's bedroom unless the child can be taught to release it in the event of fire.

Look around your home, discuss its safety shortcomings with your family, and decide what safeguards would be appropriate. Don't feel that you have to buy every gadget on the market. Buy only what you need for *your* safety situation.

An Inside Job

What do you do after you've lopped and lit and locked and bolted? Don't sit down—not yet! There are one or two—or possibly three or four—things left on your list.

- *Safe rooms.* Some safety experts recommend that every family have a "safe room" within the house or apartment. A safe room is *not* a guarded fortress, it's just an interior room (a bedroom, den, kitchen, or even bathroom) with a good lock on the door and a telephone inside. That's all. If you have a safe room and a burglar does get in, you can quietly retreat to your safe room, lock the door, and phone the police.
- *Blinds and curtains.* Remember to keep blinds and curtains closed at night so that passersby can't see in.
- *Lights.* Leave lights on in several rooms at night when you are at home alone so it won't *look* like you are alone. This may go against energy conservation rules, but the experts say it's safer.

Do you have other ideas to make your home's interior more secure? If you are still worried, there are dozens of types of burglar alarms available. Tell your family about your concern and see if they can afford one.

What about a dog—a fuzzy, four-legged burglar alarm? Well, dogs have to be fed and housebroken and walked every day. *And* they have to be trained to guard a home so that they aren't bought off by a burglar with a pound of steak. But maybe the effort is worth it for you and your family.

Some kids want to know about weapons and come up with interesting—and dangerous—ideas about what they might use as a weapon. It's very important to sort out fantasy from reality in this case.

Do you *really* think that spraying a crook with hair spray or jabbing him with a safety pin is going to discourage him from

carting off your stereo? It won't, but it will make him mad! Keep in mind, too, that chemical sprays, knives, and guns can all be wrestled away and used on *you*. If you are interested, you can take a personal defense or martial arts class. You may not become an expert, and you shouldn't use martial art skills unless you are an expert, but you will learn effective escape and self-protection skills, build your confidence, and have a great time besides.

Remember, too, you don't need adult assistance or family cooperation to develop your own safety style and practice personal and property protection. Your own habits and awareness can safeguard you *even if* your home has lousy locks, inadequate lighting, and a jungle for a front yard.

7. PROPERTY PROTECTION— Guarding Your Belongings

"My mom and I wanted to burglar-proof our apartment. The first thing we did was borrow a property engraver from the police and use it to put my mom's driver license number on the television, stereo, my mom's typewriter, and my bike. Now, if any of those things are stolen, the police can trace them back to us." —CARLOS

You can safeguard your possessions by taking a few simple precautions. Some of these suggestions require adult help, while you can do others on your own.

Take a Number

One of the best things you can do to protect your property is to mark it with an identifying number that you put on with an engraver. Many city police departments will loan you an engraver, or they are available for purchase inexpensively at hardware stores. Maybe you and your friends, club, or community Crimewatch group could make it a joint purchase!

You may want to ask an adult for help with the engraver and use a parent's social security or driver license number as the identifying number. You can either put the number in an obvious place—across the front fender of your bike or below the control panel of your television, for example—or you can put it in a more concealed location. If you choose to hide it, be sure to put a "warning" sticker in an obvious place. These stickers, which are usually available where you buy the engraver, state that the property is engraved and can be traced by police.

After you've engraved all your property, put stickers on your home's entrances warning that the property inside is marked. Thieves don't want problems. It is difficult for them to sell property that is obviously stolen, so they are likely to leave

your house and belongings alone. These stickers are also available from the police.

Keep a list of all valuable items in your home. Include a description of the item, its age, the serial number, and the identifying number engraved on it.

Some items can't be engraved but *can* be stolen. For example, can you imagine engraving a leather jacket or a down parka? Expensive clothing can and should be marked with your initials and a phone number. Use a parent's office phone or a school office phone number, but *not* your home phone number. You want to be able to get the article back if it is located, but you *don't* want to invite nuisance calls.

Ask an adult's advice about marking clothing. Sew-in or iron-on labels are one possibility, but they aren't usually big enough to discourage a thief, and they are easily cut or pulled out. If, after looking at a particular piece of clothing and an adult agrees, you might be able to write the information in large, neat letters inside the lining. This works only with a coat or jacket that is lined. Use a laundry pen.

Picture-Perfect Proof

Here's something you can do for the whole household if you have a camera.

Take snapshots of all the family treasures. Be sure to use flashbulbs or proper exposure settings for indoor photography. Get close-ups of the stereo, your bicycle, the television set, the tape deck, and anything else of value. After the pictures are developed, have an adult help you find the serial numbers of the items and record this number on the back of the appropriate picture. Now, put the whole packet in a safe place—a deposit box or the desk at a parent's office—or leave it with a trusted friend.

If your home *is* ever burglarized, or if there is a fire, you'll have "picture perfect" proof of the items you have lost to show to police, fire officials, and insurance adjusters.

Wheel Watch

Bikes require special attention. Half a million bikes are stolen *every* year! Don't let your bike become one of this year's numbers; be sure to:

- *Register it.* You have to register bikes with the police in some cities, but it's a good idea to register them even if your city doesn't require it. If your bike is stolen and later recovered by the police, they can locate you to return the bike *if* you have registered it. Call your city police department to find out what information is needed for registration and if there is a fee.

- *Engrave your bike* (see page 84). Thieves may not know that your bike is registered, but they can see an engraving mark or a "warning" sticker.

- *Invest in a good heavy-duty bike chain and a heavy padlock.* The chain should have sturdy links. The lock can be either a combination or a padlock. If you use a padlock, keep the key with your house key in a front pocket and store the spare key at home.

- *Chain and lock your bike whenever you must leave it.* Run the chain through the rear wheel and then run it through the frame once. Bring the ends of the chain through the bike rack, fence, post or whatever (strong) object you are using to "hitch it" to, and join the chain ends with your lock.

- *Wheel removal.* Some people remove the bicycle's front wheel to prevent theft. If you are concerned about theft and can safely remove your bike's front wheel, you can consider this tactic. And don't chain your front wheel to lock your bike if the wheel is removable!

- *Bike racks.* Use highly visible bike racks at schools, parks, grocery stores, or shopping centers. Lock your bike *securely* to the rack.

- *Lock it up.* Lock your bike in a garage, toolshed, or storage room when you are at home. Apartment buildings sometimes have bike racks inside the lobbies, or bicycle storage rooms, but unless your building has a doorman, your bike is probably safer in your apartment.

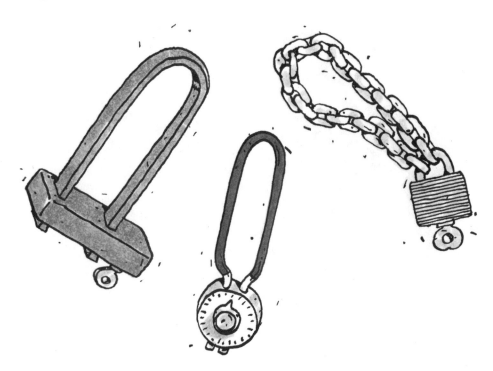

Property Protection Review

Tips about safeguarding your stuff have been given in other chapters. A few are especially worthy of review.

- *Money and valuables.* Don't take expensive property or large sums of money outside your home. If you *have* to carry either, keep it close to your body and well concealed. Don't tell anyone about it.

If you must take money or any valuable belongings to school, arrange in advance to leave them with a teacher or in the school office.

Keep your money, bus pass, and house key inside a front pocket.

- *Use good judgment when you wear jewelry.* Don't "display" your expensive or expensive-looking jewelry on buses, subways, or in crowded public places.

- *Safe carrying.* Carry your purse or bag close to your body, with the zipper or flap closed and toward your body.

- *Don't set your things down in public,* not even for "just a minute." Hold them yourself or have a friend hold them.

- *Don't turn your school locker into a "drop-in center."* Don't broadcast the combination of your locker. None of *your* friends would steal your stuff, but what about *their* friends (and their friend's cousin twice removed)?

A final reminder: If you are ever approached by anyone demanding *any* of your possessions, turn them over quickly and without a fuss! Police say that muggers are *very* rarely talked out of completing the crime and that resistance of any sort is a poor idea and could lead to a physical confrontation. Get a good look at the mugger; remember any details that might help the police identify the criminal. And phone the police as soon as possible after the crime.

8. RAPE—
Prevention
and Reporting

"No one really talks to me about rape, but I hear about it on television and see newspaper articles about it. I know kids my age are raped. I'd like to find out what I can do to keep it from happening to me."
—GINNY

The prevention tips in this book are intended to protect you from all crime, in all situations. But one crime merits special attention. Rape prevention requires extra precautions, in addition to everyday awareness and safety practices. You also need to know how to report rape and cope with the aftermath of this crime.

You might think that a chapter about rape is for girls. You might think that boys don't need to read about rape. Right? Wrong!

To begin with, boys are sometimes the victims of sexual assaults too, and many of the avoidance and response tips in this chapter can help protect them. Additionally, all concerned kids should know about rape. Effective crime prevention is a partnership of committed people, and the more people who are involved, the more effective the effort will be. While this information is presented with girls or women in the "victim" role and men in the "attacker" role, the self-protection practices work equally well for boys.

Facing Facts

Most people have a lot of incorrect ideas about rape. For example, they think of the rapist as a dirty, lonely old man in a torn trenchcoat who springs on his victims in dark alleyways.

The facts about rape are very different—and very disturbing.

1. Most rapists are between fifteen and twenty-four years of age.
2. Almost one half of all rapists are married.
3. One third of all rapes are committed by someone known to the victim.
4. Nearly one third of all rapes occur in the victim's home.

People also have old-fashioned and inaccurate notions about rape victims. They think that girls and women who are raped were somehow "asking for it," either because they wore sexy clothing or because they took careless chances (for example, hitchhiking or accepting dates with strangers).

Nothing could be farther from the truth. Girls and women are raped regardless of their age, circumstances, or "sex appeal." Rape is *not* caused by sexual desire but by anger. *The problem of rape is a problem of rapists, not a problem of rape victims.* It is not any girl's or woman's *fault* if some disturbed man chooses to vent his anger on her.

The sad fact is that *any* girl or woman of any age, appearance, or situation is a potential rape victim.

Your goal should be to decrease that potential for yourself.

Avoiding Attack

The rapist is a more dangerous criminal than either the mugger or the burglar, and you should take special efforts to protect yourself from a rapist. Here are some suggestions:

• *Don't allow yourself to be the victim of verbal assault.* Men and boys can compliment you on your appearance in a friendly, nonthreatening way. There is nothing wrong with sincere compliments. However, you should not feel flattered by loud, rude, or unwelcome comments about your looks or figure. It's not only degrading to be discussed as though you were a fold-out photograph, but it can also be dangerous. This is a method that rapists sometimes use to "check out" a victim before an actual attack.

Pretend you don't hear these comments and walk briskly away. *Don't* risk a confrontation with this type of man; why waste the time? Don't make a comment and don't answer back. Just walk away.

Another, more threatening form of assault occurs when a

man—a stranger or an acquaintance—puts his hands on you—anywhere on you—without invitation. Step quickly back from this unwelcome advance, and walk away without comment *and* without showing fear or shock. It's hard to do without practice. Try making "stone faces" into the mirror.

• *Be alert to "red lights."* If anyone—an acquaintance, employer, teacher, *whoever*—makes you uneasy by "looking you over," commenting upon your figure or appearance, touching you frequently without invitation (possibly disguising it as tickling, wrestling, etc.), discussing sex with you, or telling you "dirty" jokes, avoid that person. Walk away without comment, and if the situation continues, tell a trusted adult immediately.

- *Watch out for "intimidator-rescuer" teams when you are out in public.* This is a fairly old trick. One man or boy plays the "bad guy" and threatens you, while the other man or boy plays the "good guy" and offers to walk you somewhere or take you somewhere safe. Don't fall for this! If you are bothered in public, go to the nearest business, house, bus stop, or busy area and ask someone for help.

- *Be suspicious of strangers.* Many rapes could be avoided if girls and women would listen to their instincts about strangers and unfamiliar situations. You don't have to be scared. Just think twice—or three times—about talking to strange men, and listen *hard* to your gut feelings in unfamiliar situations.

- *If you date, know who you are dating.* If you don't know someone very well, keep your dates public. See Chapter 4 for more details.

- *Listen to your dating messages.* Are you "coming on" to a boy? *Do* you leave all arrangements up to him? Flirting is natural and usually harmless, but deliberately provocative behavior or language can be dangerous. If you *always* let a boy plan dates and control the dating situation, you are signaling your helplessness and lack of strength.

If You Are Attacked

If you are attacked, you can choose to resist—either actively or passively—or you can choose to submit. Think *now* about what you can do. You won't have time to decide in an actual attack, and you have to know what you will do *and* be prepared to do it.

Passive Resistance

Passive resistance includes such things as fainting, faking illness (gagging, choking, or pretending to have a seizure or to be mentally ill), or trying to win the attacker's sympathy and trust. If you think that you would be more comfortable using passive resistance, work up your "act" now and practice it with a friend. Once you have gone into your act in an actual attack, don't back down—commit yourself to it fully! For example, one girl was grabbed from behind at a bus stop. She immediately began praying *loudly*. Her attacker fled.

Active Resistance

Active resistance can be either verbal (power yelling or shouting) or physical (fighting back). Don't use any form of active resistance if the attacker is armed, and don't use physical resistance unless you are trained in personal defense. If you aren't trained and your efforts at escape fail, the attacker is likely to be even more angry and violent.

Verbal resistance is obviously most effective if you are in a public place where your yells will be heard and bring help, but they can be startling and effective anywhere if they are used *immediately*. An exception is when the attacker is armed; in this case, you should use only passive forms of resistance until you can plan an escape. *Good* verbal resistance is *not* screaming or pleading. It is a fierce, from-the-stomach "No! No! No!" power yell into the attacker's face. You must practice this yell (see Chapter 1).

It is important for you to understand that most rapists have a "script" for the rape. They think that you will struggle feebly at first and then cry, but you won't effectively or angrily resist them, and you will eventually submit. To effectively escape an attack, you must "rewrite" this script.

If you think that you would be comfortable fighting back, telephone your local police department to ask if it sponsors rape prevention classes. A police officer can probably direct you to one of these classes even if the police don't offer them. You can also check with the YWCA, your city park department, or private schools of martial arts or personal defense. If nothing is available locally, try to get your youth or church group, gym or health class, or neighborhood group interested in sponsoring a rape prevention class.

Decide what you would do if you were attacked. Practice whatever form of resistance you'd be most comfortable with so that if you are ever attacked, you can act quickly and decisively.

If You Are Raped

Even if you are not able to prevent a rape from occurring, you can still use your intelligence to protect yourself from further harm. You can maintain some control over the situation and help police to capture the rapist.

- *If you are being raped, remain calm and absolutely still.* Use your best judgment about continuing any sort of passive (verbal) resistance you have been using. Remind the rapist that you are a person. Tell him calmly that you are uncomfortable, that he is hurting you—make him notice *you*, not the fantasy rape victim he has in his mind.

- *Memorize as many details about the rapist that you can.* What color are his eyes, his hair? Does he have a beard, scars, a tattoo? Is he tall, short, thin, fat? What is his voice like; is it low or high? What does he say during the rape? Does he have a car—what kind is it? Does he give any clues about his name, job, or where he lives? The evidence you gather now could save many girls and women from future rapes. One woman memorized the exact shade of blue eyes of the man who raped her and knew his peculiar walk so well that when she saw him in a crowded public market a full year after the rape, she was able to summon police and direct them to him. He was later found guilty of a number of rapes and was sent to prison.

- *After the rape.* The rapist may ask you if you are going to the police or if you are going to tell anyone. Promise him that you will keep the rape a secret. Say that you just want to forget all about it. Say whatever you think the rapist wants to hear so that you can get safely and speedily away from him.

After a Rape

- *Do not bathe, shower, wash, or clean yourself off or change your clothes.* Trained doctors can gather valuable evidence from your clothes and your body.

- *Telephone the police and report the rape.* They will take you to the hospital. Or go to the hospital and have someone on the staff telephone the police. It will help you to take fast and appropriate action if you find out *now* whether your city has a hospital that specializes in treating rape victims. Does your city have a rape "hotline" number to phone in case of rape? Keep this information by your phone and keep important telephone numbers in your wallet.

- *Telephone a friend, parent, or other trusted adult to go to the hospital with you.* Have that person write down everything you can remember about the rapist and the rape. This will help you give your statement to the police and may be valuable in catching the rapist.

- *It is important to report rape to the police.* You can *not* just forget it. A very wrong thing has happened to you, and it would be unhealthy and unwise to try to brush it away. Reporting a rape helps you to deal with the understandable anger that you feel and "take charge" of your life again, as well as providing the police with information that may solve or prevent other rapes.

- *Get further help.* If you are raped, you will need to get help beyond the medical help you should get immediately. You will need counseling to help work through your anger, fear, and pain. Your friends may love you and want to help, but it may be hard for them to understand what you are going through. Phone your city's rape "hotline" and talk to your parents, school counselor, or doctor.

9. HOUSEHOLD VIOLENCE AND ABUSE— Getting Help

"I thought I was the only kid with this problem. I was ashamed to admit it. It's really a relief to find out that other kids are going through the same thing and feel the same way I feel." —ROBBIE

Not all crimes occur outside the home, and not all acts of violence are committed by strangers. It is difficult to obtain accurate figures, but it is estimated that over 100,000 kids are severely beaten each year and that at least another 50,000 are sexually abused by an adult *within their household.* Many, many more are seriously neglected or must witness a parent (usually the mother) being abused.

Domestic violence and physical and sexual abuse are painful and difficult problems. If a stranger or even an acquaintance ever abuses you or behaves violently in your presence, you will no doubt be frightened or angry. You will probably turn to a parent to receive reassurance and assistance.

But what if your attacker *is* a parent—or a grandparent or an aunt or uncle? What if the violence in your own home is more frightening than anything you would face on the street? What can you do?

Plenty! There are as many ways to control and cope with violence at home as there are to cope with violence outside the home.

Any effort to take control starts with your attitude, and attitude "adjustment" is extra-important for kids living in violent or abusive homes.

A Common Problem

First, you need to know that you are not alone. Domestic violence, child abuse, and incest occur *everywhere*—in all parts of the country and in all cities and neighborhoods. No neighbor-

hood is "safe" from this problem. It is going on *every day* in crowded city apartments, luxurious condominiums, rambling old farmhomes, and comfortable suburban houses. Abusive and violent adults are often respected members of their communities.

Think of the *hundreds of thousands* of kids caught in situations like yours. You share with them feelings of fear, anger, guilt, and confusion. You also share with them a responsibility to do something about your problem.

Getting Rid of Guilt

Next, you need to understand that you are not to blame. That may sound silly—of course you don't *ask* for a parent to hit, kick, or sexually abuse you, and of course you don't *want* your father to beat your mother—but most victims of abuse or incest, and most kids in violent homes, *do* feel guilty. They think that maybe if they had better grades or bluer eyes, their mother wouldn't hit them. They think that if they were bigger, stronger, or smarter, they would be able to protect their mother from their father. Or if only they hadn't worn that short dress, Uncle Roy wouldn't have raped them. These feelings are understandable—they are trying to make some sort of sense out of a senseless situation—but they are *wrong*. Adults who assault kids or one another do so because of *their* problems, not *your* problems.

Most abusive and violent adults are miserable. They feel so bad about themselves *as people* that it isn't possible for them to behave as confident, competent parents or grandparents (or whatever).

Their bad feelings about themselves probably started in their own childhoods. Many abusive parents were abused children; many abusive husbands grew up watching *their* fathers abuse their mothers. Abusive, violent behavior has become the behavior they understand best.

It *wouldn't matter* if you got straight As, had straight teeth, and *never* lost your lunch money. It wouldn't matter if you flirted with Grandpa or ignored him, if you stuck up for your mother or hid in a closet. If adults are abusive or violent, it is *their* problem, not yours, and their problem is likely to continue in one way or another until they get professional help.

Get rid of the guilt. Guilt won't help you make sense of the situation, but it *will* make you even more unhappy.

But what about the guilt you feel over your anger, over the fact that you sometimes *hate* your mother or father or another close relative?

That's an uncomfortable feeling, but you have a right to be angry. You have a *right* to hate someone who constantly hurts you or violates you sexually or makes your world confusing and frightening. You should *not* be hit or kicked or raped; you should *not* have to watch or listen to a parent's pain. Don't feel guilty about that anger—it is your instinct for survival. Hang on to it.

Respecting Yourself

You have a *right* to your body, and your right is not any less than that of an adult. You don't "owe" anyone sexual favors; it is not the "right" of a parent or another adult to hit you; you *should* be able to enjoy your life free from fear. You are en-

titled to peace of mind, sexual privacy, and freedom from pain.

You have a *responsibility* to yourself. You should not allow yourself to be tricked into sexual activity with an adult. It is far more common for an adult to bribe or shame a kid into having sex than to force it. You have a responsibility to stop the physical abuse to yourself—and your younger brothers and sisters—and a responsibility to help a parent trapped in a violent marriage.

That may be hard for you to accept, especially if you have been caught in a difficult situation for a long time. If you have been, your confidence has been damaged, and you feel incompetent after all the months or years of helplessness.

But look at those months or years. Look at how long you have lived with this problem. It takes a huge amount of strength, skill, and intelligence just to *survive* abusive and violent homes. If you have survived it, you have proven that you have the strength to change it.

Getting Help

If you are being beaten or sexually abused at home, you will have to tell someone. There are lots of choices. You can tell:

A parent (if you are being abused by the other parent)
Another close relative
A family friend whom you trust
A church leader or youth group leader
A school counselor or teacher
A friend's parent or a trusted adult neighbor
A doctor

You must decide in advance who to tell, what you will say (write it down, even rehearse it if that helps you), and who *else* you will tell if the first person doesn't believe you or does not help you.

Sometimes, parents or relatives are so upset and frightened to learn that another parent or relative has abused you that they may refuse to discuss it, they may deny it, or they may even blame *you*. You have to understand that they are speaking from their own fear and confusion. If this happens to you, drop the subject and tell someone else.

If you don't know anyone you can tell or if you don't get help from the person you do tell, there are many agencies and organizations that can help you. Here are some ideas:

• *Crisis or abuse "hotlines."* Look in your telephone book in the directory's Community Services section or under a specific organization such as Parents Anonymous. Call and ask for help.

- *Agencies.* Look for the Child Welfare League or the Society for the Prevention of Cruelty to Children in your phone book. For community mental health clinics or centers, check city or county listings in your phone book. And your state's Department of Public Welfare or Department of Social Service is under state agency listings in the phone book.

- *Clinics.* These include drop-in clinics, the child guidance or pediatric sections of hospitals, or county public health clinics. Check hospital or county listings. You can call the hospital number and say you wish to report a child abuse problem.

- *Police.* You can also go to the police. If you decide to do this, try to contact a juvenile officer or counselor. They've had experience in dealing with kids, and you will probably be comfortable talking to them.

- *Alateen.* You can also contact Alateen, a division of Alcoholics Anonymous. Look in your phone book under Alcoholics Anonymous. Alateen was founded for the children of alcoholics and is used to help kids living in very difficult situations. While Alateen might not be able to help you with your particular problem, it will be able to guide you to someone who can.

You should realize that an abuse problem can't be cured overnight. Abusive parents or relatives will need counseling or therapy to solve their problems, and you will need therapy to help "heal" the emotional damage that has been done. You may even need to be separated from your family for a time while you both work out your individual problems. It won't be easy. You will still have hard work ahead of you. However,

getting help is an important first step. By telling someone, you've gone a long way toward taking control of your life.

If your mother is being abused, you need to help her help herself. Tell her that you love her and want to assist her. Remember, months or years of abuse have left her feeling helpless, frightened, and depressed. She will require a lot of support from you. If she wants to get help and has no family members, friends, or church officials to turn to, give her the following information:

- *Shelters.* Many cities have shelters for battered women and their children. Check the Community Services section of your telephone directory or telephone the National Organization for Women (NOW) or the YWCA to find out if shelters are available in your community.

- *Health centers.* Help is available from community mental health centers and some women's health clinics.

- *Alcoholics Anonymous* can help if your abusive parent has a drinking problem, and it can direct you and your mother to other sources of assistance.

It is not uncommon for a woman to be "paralyzed" by abuse. She is terrified by what is happening, but she has no confidence in herself. She often has no money or job skills, and she is as frightened of trying to make it on her own as she is of continuing in her present situation.

What should you do if your mother refuses to get help and the violence continues?

- *Get help for yourself.* Talk to a school counselor, teacher, church official, club leader, adult friend, or relative.

- *Be honest about your home situation.* It's tempting to deny it, or to exaggerate it. Many kids build up a "fantasy family" that in no way resembles the confused, frightened, fighting family they *really* have. Don't lie to yourself. Don't tell yourself that your family is any better or any worse than it really is.

- *Join Alateen or another club or organization.* The advantage of Alateen is that the other kids have home situations as difficult as yours, or even worse.

- *Get on with your life.* Take a class, join a team, make a friend, or get a part-time job. Build a life for yourself *away* from home. It will get you out of the house and will give you something positive to hold on to.

- *Don't get directly involved in your parents' fights.* Go to another room, but *don't* take sides. If you must phone the police, do so quietly so that you don't become a target too.

In all these instances—physical or sexual abuse or other domestic violence—it is essential that you face the situation and do *everything possible* to get help.

Reaching Out

If you have a friend you think is being abused, sexually violated, or severely neglected at home, you have a responsibility to get help for your friend, *even if* he or she does not ask for help. Abuse victims can become so defeated by their situation that they have trouble seeking help. As a friend, and as a kid concerned with crime prevention, you *must* tell a parent, school counselor, teacher, or other trusted adult. Remember, effective crime prevention depends upon people caring about and protecting one another as well as caring about and protecting themselves.

10. SAFE-KEEPING— The Last Word in Crime Prevention

Your involvement in crime prevention can't stop when you complete this book, and it shouldn't fade a month from now when you are busy with new activities and other concerns. Crime prevention can't be put on the shelf and brought out in "dangerous situations." By now, safety practices should be an everyday thing for you, as much a part of your life as your respect for yourself.

Don't take your safety for granted. Remain alert to changes in yourself, your community, and your home. How's the crime rate in your neighborhood? Is it going up, or are neighborhood Crimewatch efforts paying off in reduced crime rates? Do you need to adjust any of your safety practices in the light of the current situation? Do you or family members have any new purchases that need to be engraved or photographed? Is your new birthday bike registered and engraved? Do you have a sturdy chain and a good lock for it? Do you remember to use it? Have the hedges around your home grown back, blocking doorways or windows and making it difficult for neighbors to watch your home?

How are *you* doing? Are you walking tall, speaking clearly and with confidence? Do you watch where you go, what you wear, and what you carry with you when you leave home? Would you pass the "safety savvy" tests in Chapter 2 if you took them today?

You've learned that there are many, many ways that you can protect yourself, your home, and your belongings, but these methods are only as good as your determination to use them. To stay safe, you must play it safe—for keeps.

Safety Sources

Abuse

What to Read

Hunt, Irene. *The Lottery Rose.* New York: Charles Scribner's Sons 1976. When Georgie Burgess goes to live in a home for boys, he begins to build a new life, one based on love and friendship rather than the fear and suspicion that years of abuse have caused. Fiction.

Roberts, Willo Davis. *Don't Hurt Laurie!* New York: Atheneum 1980. Laurie and her mother move around; the one thing that remains constant in Laurie's life is her mother's abuse of her. Laurie's pain and fear and need for love come to life in this touching novel. Fiction.

Where to Get Help

Help for abuse problems can often be provided by adult friends or relatives, schools (teachers or counselors), churches (ministers or youth leaders), or adult leaders of youth groups (such as Scouts, YMCA, YWCA, or YMHA). In addition to these sources of help, many communities have agencies that deal with abuse. The following list is only partial; different communities provide different help under a variety of different names.

- Telephone "hotlines." Crisis lines of any type will provide advice.
- Parents Anonymous.
- Child Protective Society.
- Child Welfare Committee.
- The Child Welfare League.
- American Humane Association (Children's Division).
- Community (or County) Mental Health. Look under city or county listings.

- Community (or County) Family or Youth Services. Look under city or county listings.
- County (or State) Department of Social Services. Look under county or state listings.
- Hospitals, clinics, doctor's offices.
- Police, juvenile officers.

Alcoholism

What to Read

Hornik, Edith Lynne. *You and Your Alcoholic Parent: A Young Person's Guide to Understanding and Coping.* New York: Association Press 1974.
This straightforward book provides general information about alcohol use and abuse and gives recommendations for action in specific alcohol-related situations ranging from handling tension and conflict within the family to coping with the social problems of having an alcoholic parent.

Seixas, Judith S. *Living With a Parent Who Drinks Too Much.* New York: Greenwillow Books 1979.
A book to help kids understand their alcoholic parent *and* understand themselves and the problems caused by their parent's drinking. The book gives good concrete advice, including advice on how and where to seek help.

Where to Get Help

As with abuse, help with alcohol-related problems can often be obtained from adult friends and relatives, teachers and counselors, church and youth group leaders, or other trusted adults. The community or county mental health offices and family or youth services agencies listed under the abuse section may also give assistance or referral. Additionally, there are government and private organizations that deal with alcoholism. Look for the following, or related, listings in the telephone book.

- Alcoholics Anonymous. A.A. has a youth division, Alateen, for the children of alcoholics.

- Alcohol Information Center (city, county, or state).
- Council on Alcoholism (city, county, or state).

Crime Prevention

What to Read

Many excellent pamphlets are available free, or for a small fee, from government agencies. Check with your local police or sheriff's department or request crime prevention information from: Superintendent of Documents, U.S. Government Printing Office, Washington, DC 20402.

Where to Get Help

- Check with the local police or sheriff for information about neighborhood crime prevention groups *and* for home safety inspection (if this service is available in your area).
- Police (or public libraries) sometimes have property engravers to loan.

Rape

What to Read

Here are two useful books that examine myths about rape, provide insights into the reality of the crime, and give sound advice on both rape prevention and dealing with the effects of rape.

Bode, Janet. *Rape; Preventing It; Coping With the Legal, Medical and Emotional Aftermath.* New York: Franklin Watts 1979.

Booher, Dianna D. *Rape: What Would You Do If. . . ?* New York: Messner 1981.

Where to Get Help

- *Prevention.* Local police departments, YWCA, women's organizations, and Scouting groups offer rape prevention classes in some communities.
- *Aftermath.* Many communities have a rape "hotline." If your community has one, keep the telephone number handy, both at home and in your billfold when you are away.

If there is no rape hotline, telephone the police in the event of rape or go to the hospital.

To obtain counseling after a rape, telephone a women's health center, speak to your family doctor, or telephone community or county mental health offices.

Self-Defense

What to Read

There are many books available showing personal defense or martial arts techniques, and any of them would provide interesting background reading. But it is important to remember that these skills should be learned and tested in a "classroom" situation before you can rely upon them as personal protection.

Where to Get Help

Many organizations teach self defense. Try:

- Police (probably taught as rape prevention)
- City Parks Department
- Community colleges
- Scouts
- YMCA, YWCA, YMHA
- Private schools of martial arts and/or self-defense

Index

Kathy S. Kyte

is the author of *In Charge: A Complete Handbook for Kids with Working Parents*, a companion volume to *Play It Safe*. She has also written newspaper feature articles, fiction and poetry. She was born in Reno, Nevada, grew up in Eugene, Oregon, and graduated with a B.S. degree in communications and journalism from Lewis and Clark College in Portland, Oregon.

Ms. Kyte lives with her husband and her two children in Iowa City, Iowa.